Masks of the Muse

Building a Relationship with the Goddess of the West

Masks of the Muse

Building a Relationship with the Goddess of the West

by Veronica Cummer

PENDRAIG PUBLISHING, LOS ANGELES

Pendraig Publishing, Sunland, CA 94040
© Veronica Cummer 2009. All rights reserved.
Published 2009.
Printed in the United States of America
ISBN 978-0-9820318-3-4

"The third type of possession and madness is possession by the Muses. When this seizes upon a gentle and virgin soul it rouses it to inspired expression in lyric and other sorts of poetry, and glories countless deeds of the heroes of old for the instruction of posterity. But if a man comes to the door of poetry untouched by the madness of the Muses, believing that technique alone will make him a good poet, he and his sane compositions never reach perfection, but are utterly eclipsed by the performances of the inspired madman."

Socrates

"I never know when I sit down, just what I am going to write. I make no plan; it just comes, and I don't know where it comes from."

D. H. Lawrence

Table of Contents

Dedication

Brightest blessings come upon you
By the love of She who walks the night,
By the heart
Of the Queen of the sea;
The grace of Her hand and Her form
Be laid upon you,
As naked once She rose from foam
And stood,
A pearl within a hooded shell.

In my first book, I thanked the Gods and Goddesses who have served to inspire the words upon the page and graced me with Their thoughts and feelings and poetry and insights and desires. I also gave my thanks to the Muse, a gratitude that must also extend to this work.

But then it seems only fitting, especially in a book that not only reflects the result of years of interaction and communion with the Muse, but is actually about the powers of inspiration and creativity. A book that is about the Muse or, at least, a few of Her faces, since She has as many forms as there are worlds, artists, dreamers, and visionaries to imagine them.

This time around, though, I also want to take the time to thank a few others who have aided and abetted me on this path, who have stood by me and provided encouragement through good times and bad, trial and triumph, challenges of ecstasy and ordeal. Those who once stood with me upon that terrible precipice and also chose of their own volition to jump when jumping was called for, to go through the door that you cannot *un*choose once it has been chosen.

Thank you, thank you, thank you to my Brothers and Sisters both near and far…may the Arts inspire and fulfill you. Thanks also to those who provided an example and were always there with good advice and support, even if sometimes that advice and support took the form of letting people make up their own minds and go their own way. All my love and respect to my Queen and Magus, a dedicated couple who have offered up years of their lives in blessed service to the Craft. They've always been there with good advice, kindness, acceptance and above all, more compassion than I've ever been capable of.

Certainly, my blessing and thanks must go to those who also have come to stand with me as fellow children of the Muse and for which I cannot thank Her enough…Alexei, Chris, "Lightning Boy," Jack, John, Sheldon, Mort, and the Candy Man, who speaks in the language of riddles and sweet paradox.

Finally, to give credit where credit is due, my thanks also to those who walked and guided me a good ways along this path, only to face a parting at the last that hopefully has imparted as much strength as it did pain, and that will lead back to joy again in time. Thank you and good luck to my first teachers and to my youngest sister, may you all find what you are looking for and be the better for it.

Preface

"I am not the mother of ideas, but the midwife. If you must call me anything at all, call me that. Yet remember it is not I who names things nor gives them form, but you. They are as much of you as they are of me, if not more so. Do not blame me if they do not turn out how you would have liked, for I did not choose how they would manifest. You did that. Knowingly or unknowingly, and you can guess which occurs more often. Open your eyes. You make the world. What do you want it to be? You are yet children, but children who must grow up. Not all of us adore children. I do not, and so I am not your mother nor the mother of your world. Call me mother if you like, it will not make it true or make you one of mine. Only your promise of service can do that, but never take such a promise lightly for I will not."

The Goddess of the West, the Muse

This book was begun before the last was finished, though in many ways it has been spiraling towards existence for a good decade or more. It's part of an ongoing process of building a relationship with the Goddess of the West, She who is also the Muse. When She first showed up we didn't know Her name, but only saw how direct She could be—right in your face was the phrase that sometimes came to mind after dealing with Her—so that some people even felt She was a touch cruel at times. However, that was our fear talking, our lack of understanding. We have since come to realize otherwise for, above all, the Muse *is* emotion, all the good, all the bad, the joys and sorrows, ecstasy and anguish. As She is beauty past the common understanding of the mind, a beauty akin to the naked touch of the Divine, a touch that can burn.

It was on the shore of a northern lake that She first began to reveal to us who She was and why She was here. I can still remember that night—the warm night air, the slightly citrus smell of the flames from the four torches we had lit, citronella to try and keep the mosquitoes at bay, and how clearly the stars were reflected in the still black waters of the lake. The moon was nearly full, but somehow Her light didn't entirely seem to penetrate the night very deeply. A loon called from the black and another answered, a high and haunting sound that seemed to come from everywhere and nowhere.

The Goddess we eventually knew as the Goddess of the West showed up. She gave us four of Her names that night and more later, but it's those four first names that I've concentrated on and worked to make a connection to in order to write about Her. Of those names, the coven I was in chose at the last to call Her Ariadne, while another coven decided to use Cerridwen, instead. She remained the same Goddess deep down, yet the choice of name subtly altered both Her aspect and the relationship with each group.

We didn't know then where that Goddess and that night would lead us, but as the Muse is emotion and inspiration, creation and destruction, always moving, going, doing, it proved neither an easy nor a particularly safe road. But it did show us a lot, not the least being the strength of our own hearts and the necessity of focused intention. We also learned the price paid for passion and the power of faith, not blind faith as the Christians sometimes teach it, but faith tied to will and so persuasive of Fate Herself.

The strange thing is that, for myself, I feel Her presence most deeply in a name that came much, much later—that of *Marisse*, a Goddess of the sea, of blood, and of the flowers born of blood, the rose and the violet. She has charmed her way into my life and taught me many things, despite the difficulties of language between us. She may only speak old French, yet we have found common purpose together all the same.

So to Ariadne, to my Marisse, this work is dedicated as a poem of praise, a hymn of honest gratitude. As a writer, I cannot by any means ignore She who is the mask of that electric current of

12

inspiration. I cannot deny what needs to be acknowledged and that is that without the Muse the page remains blank and the canvas bare. Without the Muse the fields grow fallow and the table remains empty. Without the Muse the bees will not come to the bloom, if even the flowers blossom. Without the Muse, what is life and where, where can we find beauty? Without the Muse, who among us would dare to wish for more, let alone will to make it happen…

To the Goddess of the West, then, is given the poetry in this book, the prose, and the rituals. Rituals meant to be Her rituals and to help provide a way for us to contact Her—whichever aspect is preferred—and begin to walk a path of conscious creation. As a side note, the rites were written primarily for group use, but most of them can be adapted for solitaries if required. They can be used in conjunction with whatever path is normally followed and can be embellished as required. We all have within us our own expression of the Art and though some of us work together, sharing a common purpose, we yet remain prophets of our own reality, servants of love and magick.

Introduction

Hymn to the Muse

Fading blue light
And gone
Her hair is black as night
And binds me round
As ink might in serpentine words
The tongue of the snake flickers
And poems form and fade
Seafoam pain
And tides of birds on the rise
White birds and black
Red birds and grey
My feet carry me onwards
Into the dusk
The dawn
The day
Her pen is sharp as a blade
Her voice a dream

Who is the Muse? Where does inspiration come from? What place do the Arts have in our lives? Why do some stories move us more than others? Why do some of them even have the ability to affect and transform our lives, causing us to go off in pursuit of something unknown, strange, exotic, even dangerous. To give up all we have to try to attain something we can barely glimpse, but that it seems as though we have long dreamed about. That great unknown something *more*.

The Muse is mysterious and beautiful, terrifying and desirable. She has been talked about, written about, dramatized, painted and sculpted, worshipped and feared down through countless generations of human history. Sometimes, She has been given Her due as a Goddess. At other times, Her true face has been hidden away from the sight of mere mortals or She has been named a devil, a temptress, a sorceress, a Witch. She is many things to many people and has altered with our perception and expectation of Her, though at heart She remains inspiration—what inspires us to good or evil, to beauty or to ugliness.

Historically, we tend to think of there being nine Muses, a legacy of ancient Greece. But, that change only came about in later times. Earlier, there was a Triple Muse and the aspects of this Triple Muse were *Song*, *Meditation*, and *Memory*, with Memory being the most important of them all. Meditation is an altered state of awareness, either of the universe around us or of our own internal universe or both, one where we are fixed and focused. Memory is, obviously, what we remember, but not just with our minds, as memory also resides in our bodies, our blood, our spirits, and the shared awareness of our kind. We remember the past, but we can remember the future, as well, for time is not linear. Only our unviable belief that the past is set in stone and the future fluid and as yet unwritten keeps us from memory of all. The truth is that all is stone and all is fluid, both at the same time, if you pardon the expression.

We can fix our attention, remember what was, what is, what will be, and use this to sing up the world. Song *is* creation, even more than the word. Song is an intrinsic part of group gatherings and rituals going back before humans were even humans. Song can bind us together as it also binds the universe together—the song of vibration, of living spirit and energy, of the inter-relationship of all things. What is a song but sung emotion and what is emotion but memory tied to feeling? When all three of these aspects are woven together, focused, they can work magick. They can heal or harm. They become spells and charms, capable of making changes or keeping the same what has already begun.

When the Muse became nine in number, they were called the daughters of Zeus. Apollo or Helios, the Greek God of the Sun, was given authority over the Arts and became their mentor. In particular, He took over the authority of the Art of healing and

16

medicine. But what this reveals is more of a metaphor than a mere transfer of power. It shows us the close relationship of the Muses to both the sun, which is the visual representation of fire and of the light of creation, and to the lightning—Zeus's dread thunderbolt—which links the sky to the earth, the realm of the Gods to the land of men.

This divine lightning bolt is, after all, the sudden strike and supernatural force of inspiration and originates with the *source* of inspiration, a power that remains the provenance of the Mansions of Night and of the Muse, no matter how many faces She may choose to wear. Just as the ecstasy that Her power brings remains a gift to those who seek Her out and wish to serve the Arts.

We plug into this power through the Muse and let it surge through us, bringing with it gifts of joy and pleasure, of change and necessity. We *create*...but what we create doesn't truly come to life without the Muse and, for that if for nothing else, She should be acknowledged. One way we can do this is by letting the world see Her true beauty through the very acts of creation that we make, no matter the form they may take. Through engaging and immersing ourselves in the Arts—giving ourselves over to that pure power flowing through us, giving it a window into this world—we show that the Muse is as beloved of us as we are beloved of Her. We come to understand that by being a portal for the Arts that we couldn't get there without Her or, if we did, that life just wouldn't have that special sparkle that we long so for and admire.

There is no clear agreement over particular Arts the Nine Muses are in charge of, but in general Calliope's powers are over epic poetry, stories of Gods and heroes, of Kings and grand aspirations. To Erato is bequeathed erotic poetry and the Art of the mime, both given to the movement and beauty of the body. Urania is about the gift of astrology, not the least being the nature of destiny and the workings of Fate. Calliope means "beautiful face," though, perhaps a more accurate interpretation might be the "face of beauty." Erato's

17

name means the "beloved one," and Urania is the "one of heaven." If you put all three together, another triple power emerges—that of Beauty, Desire, and the Heavens. Certainly, that describes not just a Goddess of eroticism and pleasure, but also a Queen of Heaven and of Earth. Not to forget that we desire what we find beautiful and those desires and what they inspire us to be and to do can be found within the stories of the stars, within our own stories.

To the other six daughters of Zeus—Clio, Euterpe, Thalia, Melpomene, Polyhymnia, and Terpsichore belong the aspects of history, lyric poetry, comedy, tragedy, hymns and religious dance, and choral singing and dancing. If it all seems just a little too pat, it probably is, for much of the wildness, the sheer poetic madness of inspiration was lessened and downplayed by breaking up the Muse into such civilized aspects.

Still the Muse can't be tamed, even if you succeed in handing over the majority of Her power to another God. However, it must be said that the God *was* Apollo, a deity once far less civilized than he is normally thought of today. In actuality, His healings were performed in the dark, by undergoing an almost literal rebirth from disease and resurrection from the tomb. This makes sense for the gold of the Muse is related to creation, a creation symbolized by the visible light of the sun, the part that normally is all we can see. This gold lies hidden in the earth, in the darkness, and there we must seek it, whether for healing or for magick.

Some old religions equate the sun to a masculine power and the moon to a feminine one, but that's just one way of looking at the dynamic interplay and connection of "opposites." One is of the light—symbol of the source of the greater light—and the other is of the reflection, the glimmering shadow face, of that same light. One is the mirror and the other the gate. Except that mirrors can be gates and gates can be mirrors. But, in order for a mirror to be a gate, it must be unblemished. It needs to be polished and purified.

Otherwise, what you see in it, what comes through it, is less than what it can and should be; it cannot reflect the true light properly.

The sun can be seen as a metaphor, a mirror of the true gold, the glorious Divine power that pours into and through the universe— particles of pure love. Apollo is thus a God who represents the Seen power as opposed to the Unseen one which lies behind it, even though He too has his beginnings in the rich and fertile darkness. From that same fertile dark springs the powers of the Muse, just as the dark gives rise to the solar Phoenix. We have to make sure that our mirrors are bright and clear in order to let this golden light pass through us and into what we create to contain it. As what comes from the Unseen flows into the Seen and makes it flower.

Sunlight gives life and energy, but that's not all that's necessary to make life living. This gold, this life, this creative energy, lies hidden in all things, a treasure waiting to be found, a fire waiting to be stirred to life. We may have to dig to find it, but it's well worth the effort in the end for we all can be gates and mirrors for inspiration and creation, the same way the Mirror-Muse is. The sun is a poem to this power of the Muse, a power that is shaped into many things and projects itself out into existence, into the world that we recognize as our own. The sun that we can see actually stands in the place of the power which we can't see, at least not with Earthly vision. For to see that other light requires what is commonly known as the Second Sight. This Unseen light is the "white sun" spoken of in alchemy, a symbol of the One Mind, the great consciousness that is the Ultimate Source.

Thus, Apollo is lord of the sun and of the nine Muses, the dancing ladies of poem and of praise, but He is still only a visual reference point for the far greater force behind Him, a power that cannot enter into our world in its entirety. Certainly, it would burn us up if we attempted it, just as Semele—the mother of Dionysus—was blinded and burnt and died to her earthly existence when Zeus reluctantly appeared to her in His true form. She was turned to ashes by the Divine presence that is the Divine's purest nature. In order to avoid this for ourselves, we must catch and bring into our world bits and pieces of the Divine that we can create suitable masks for. We bring something real to life in the end, yet it remains a mask.

The moon is sister and echo of the sun, as the huntress Goddess Artemis was twin sister to Apollo. This mirror, this moon, this mask, is how that light comes into our world, by taking on a reflection of its own self. Through the moon we may view the sun, or at least a more bearable aspect of its light. It's kind of like only being able to see something by peering at it out of the corner of your eye. When you face it directly, you can't see it anymore because it blinds you or fools you much in the way of Faery. But when you look sidelong into the mirror and don't forget that you look into a mirror—because if you forget you might get lost in the reflection and start thinking that what you're looking at is the real thing—then you might manage to catch a glimpse of what lies beyond the mask.

The moon and the sun, just as light and dark, night and day, is a metaphor for the dual nature of the universe and how that duality makes up a whole. The sun represents the life force and the moon the way we can perceive that life force, though the ever-changing masks it takes on. In a pool, a pond, a lake, a river, a stream, and, most of all, in the great wide oceans of the world, we may catch sight of one of those masks, the mutable and transmuting Muse. She is in the blackest currents at the bottom of the sea, the dark undreamt of fantastical horrors that both fascinate and repel us. She is in the flicker and flash of sunlight on the morning waves. She is in the white-plumed crash of the surf upon the shore, upon the broken rocks of desire. Just as She is the mermaid upon those rocks, combing out her long wet hair, the Siren, the Lorelei, the temptress and maiden and cruel mother and monster of the sea.

But pools, rivers, bogs, and wells can be gateways to the land of the dead as well as to poetry and vision. Tolkien's elves passed not so much into the land of the West as into the blessed realms of those who have for a time completed their journey and work upon the earthly shores. The isle of Avalon also is said to lie across the Western seas, the resting place of Arthur and of the apples of the sun. It is no coincidence that the West is equated to gleaming islands of new promise, to that which rises up from the sea and makes a new world. Nor to the mist that is emblem of the Veil that surrounds us and may sometimes part to reveal strange visions, even the lonely shores where the glorified dead reside.

The West is a way to the Otherworld. It's water and emotion and daring. To the West lies dusk, twilight, the setting sun, the evening star, and the sea. Small wonder that the Muse and water and emotion share many attributes, capable of being both beautiful and terrible in equal measure, and always, always dangerous. Like the sea that sailors down through history have both loved and feared in equal measure, the Muse is changeable and moody, generous one moment and capable of cruelty the next.

Yet, though the sea is capricious, Her waters are also bountiful and her depths contain treasures beyond measure. For the sea also represents the great unknown Void, the one we must seek to traverse if we are to go beyond all that we know or think that we know and seek after greater treasures, some of which we can't hardly even conceive of. We cannot hope to grasp these treasures of the depths unless we dare the journey and are, ourselves, changed by all that we have endured. We cannot bring them back and give rise to their creation unless we know what it is that we desire them to be.

We honor the Muse through this act of creation but also by way of fascination. To be fascinated by something, to make something fascinating, that's all a part of Her worship. If you are a writer and the words come in that perfect rush of power, then they are your praise to Her, your poem, your prayer, your hymn. You invoke Her through Her own Art, through the Art that you share with Her, which then takes on a life and power of its very own, fascinating others, charming them if you will.

For the past 2000 years or more, the Muse has given freely and unstintingly of this gift without a request of proper recompense. Accordingly, during the Age of Pisces, we did not need to give due even though due was owed. The current of inspiration was free for all, despite a lack of acknowledgement of the mask who granted a door into that current. Thanks or praise or even acknowledgement of the Muse was not required, though it would have been right to do so.

However, that time is done for the Age of Pisces is spent and falling into decay, the great wheel of the heavens spinning towards Aquarius. In fact, in some ways, the skies and the Age have already turned, enough that the acceptability of not giving the Muse Her due is no longer true. There will be no more free rides. During the Age of Aquarius, we will have to thank the Muse for Her gifts or else we will inevitably find ourselves cut off from that creative flow, from the source of inspiration. We will find it increasingly difficult to bring anything back from the Source, to bring something new into existence.

Gratitude is the watchword of the world now, gratitude and reciprocity. Without which, the coffers will grow empty, the well run dry, and we will all grow hungry and thirsty, not just for what we need to nourish our bodies but the food and drink our hearts and souls require. We may be able to continue to write, to paint, to dance, to sing, to take photographs, to perform ritual, but it will never be as good as it can be, as good as it should be. None of it will reach that epitome that some might call magick. It may be decent, even good, but never great. It may be able to touch others a little, but it won't have the sheer power of transformation.

If you have ever found yourself staring at a blank and mocking page, an empty canvas, you know this hunger already. You know what it feels like to try and try again to get something the way you instinctually feel it needs to be in order to be good, to be brilliant, to shine, only to fail again and again to be spectacular, to be brilliant. It seems as though it is right there, just beyond the reach of your fingertips, that you can almost touch it…yet it doesn't come, it doesn't flow, it just isn't *right*.

Worse still, the gift of the Muse does not just involve what are normally thought of the Arts such as singing or dancing, writing, painting and acting, just to name a few examples. Her gift suffuses many more aspects of our lives, for *anything* that we do and do well—marvelously well—is because of Her grace. So it is not just what is commonly known as the Arts which will be effected in the Age of the Water-Bearer, but everything from sports to public speaking to teaching to giving advice to making love, even to throwing a party or a charity event. You name it, if you want to do it well and not just adequately, if you want it to take on a life of its own, then you need the Muse.

What is the legacy you wish to leave? What is the mark you mean to make? For what do you want to be remembered? For though we linger in people's memories, even that fades with time unless people tell stories of us and those tales are passed down. Unless we leave behind bits of ourselves in all that we create. Because as our creations continue, we continue with them. These creations are our children in a way, whether literal or figurative ones. They are gifts to us, gifts made for us to nurture and to, eventually, present to the larger world. They are given to us through the auspices of the Muse and we are *meant* to pass them along, to continue the cycle, transforming not just us, but those around us who we come into contact with.

It can eventually even harm us if we don't keep the current going, if we don't do our part in the ever-renewing and continuing cycle, for such energies are not meant to be kept. For one thing, inspiration can destroy and devour as much as create and inspire. It can harm as much as heal. Like a double-edged blade or herbs that can cure or kill, the greater powers always have two aspects to them. The force behind the mask of the Muse is no different; She is beautiful and She is terrible, just as is all that we can create through Her.

This book contains four masks of the Muse, four names that represent Goddesses who are slightly different aspects of the power of the West, of water and emotion and daring and inspiration. Those names are Aphrodite, Cerridwen, Ariadne, and the Lady of the Lake. Each of Them have provided Their own words, Their own insights, and separate yet complimentary viewpoints on inspiration and the Arts which are at Their command and at our service. Though, of course, now it comes at a price.

This book is part of paying that price, of looking into the mirror, of seeking ecstasy in the dark, in the light, in the burning kiss of the Divine.

Pledge to the Muse

Dark mother Muse
Dread and wild
I cannot resist you
I won't even try
Take me
Hurt me
Consume me
I am yours
Give me of your passion
One kiss devouring
Marked by blood
Set on fire
I am as ash
Nothing more
Nothing less

Mute and forlorn
Lost upon the shore
Of unquiet shades
What grey day
My hour of hunger
Forever dim
These but my chains
Pain
Doubt
Shame
I cannot bear them
I must be free
I must rise
I shall die to be

So I ask of you
Dread Muse

I beg you
Dark Queen
Let me fly again
A phoenix flame
To worship divine
Your face
Your dance
The dream

Lend me strength
Heal me
Conceive me
I am yours
As I will to surrender
Blood
Ash
Bone
Longing to be devoured
Devouring my own
Breathless
Song beyond joy
Beyond death
The stolen flame
My name

Part One
Aphrodite

Daughter of Pleasure

Sea born
Your hair is foam
Cradling you from the deeps
Keeping you close
As your secret name forgotten
You drift for two thousand years or more
Before washing up on the shore at last
The sun warm upon cool skin
Naked flesh pale and golden
You breathe for the first time in forever.

The air stings
And one tear falls for the pain
Sweet and salt a crystal jewel
Diamond and pearl and true
It traces passage down your cheek
To lie forlorn upon the sand below
Until a bird desiring of its gleam
Cautiously wheels and dives down
To steal it
A bird once white but now black
Burned by its own passage
By all of life desired
The narrow strand between joy and pain.

You don't wake
For dreams are still too precious to forsake
Besides what's one poor lost gem
When a thousand more yet lie inside
Tears enough for a generation
For an age
One that only believes in monsters
And not pretty girls spread upon the sand

Deep water wanton
Dangerous and glad
And though they don't know your name yet
They shall
Though few will choose to remember
That beneath your beauty
As beneath the waves
Lies the terrible strength
The consuming hunger
The hopeless hurting praise
Of sunken ship and city
Of monster and of maid.

Your footsteps fill with perfume
Fragrant red and gold and pearl
A burning song
A track of golden fire
As you wake at long last
And begin to walk these shores as yet unknown
Choosing your way between land and tide
Your face your form your smile
The face and form and dream
The breathless expression of desire
Forgotten no more but called
Back from the depths
Which once gave them name
For the sake of those who would love
And in the loving fear.

The sun was white, golden, red, luminous and strange. It was the light of rebirth, of resurrection, of the beginning of something eternally new, something never yet known. Motes of light cascaded across the waters, glimmered on the waves, dusting the distant sands of the islands that lay scattered through the expanse of breathless sea like the pearls lost from some ancient necklace. The whole world held its breath and waited, knowing with an instinctual awareness that something was coming, something marvelous and mysterious and necessary.

The waters were dark at first, save for the glow of the dawn upon them. But the light soon chased the dark away, both above and below. The sea turned blue, blue-green, and then clear enough to glimpse what lay in the depths below. One secret rose up from that place, passing from blackness into the blue-green waters above. As it rose it took on a form, a shape, a name long awaited. No mere whisper of the sea, but a splendid song, a whisper of tides and of dreams as yet undreamt of. No mere nymph, no simple daughter of the Lord of the Waves, but all that may be known of love while in the flesh.

Birds rose and darted through the sky overhead, weaving out patterns that were messages, songs and prayers. They were the first to see Her, to know Her, to watch as She appeared from the waters, weaving form from the white foam drifting on the waves. Pale and perfect, one hand, one arm, emerged into the air above, long fingers tangled in a net, clutching a shell. It was followed by a swirl of hair, black at first and then red and finally sun-gold, hair that streamed longer than her body. Her upper body was that of a woman, but mid-way it merged into a fish's tail, thin silver scales shimmering in the sun with a thousand dazzling colors.

Her eyes were closed as she floated upon water and foam and weed above the blue-green waters, a dream of sleep, a dream of awakening, a dream of men's desire. She lay in stillness as the currents carried Her where they would, drifting towards that distant white-sand shore. When at the last, the sea gave Her up to the land's embrace, it was gently, sorrowfully, as though reluctant to let go. But as the sun's light fell more fully on Her the scales began to loosen and fall away, turning into pearls, into amber, moonstone, topaz, amethyst, emerald, and gems as yet unnamed. Long legs were revealed, lush hips, lush enough to give birth to a world.

She slept as though one not yet truly alive, even as a small, plain brown sparrow alighted a few steps from Her and carefully hopped closer and closer. A dove landed on the other side of Her, peering intently with black eyes. Had they seen Her before? Did they know this sleeping Goddess?

Despite this being the moment of Her birth, they both did know Her for She was the form upon the prow of every ship, the one who led the way. Hers was the dance beneath each swirling veil, the one to show the way. Hers was the dream that poets sought and which men hungered and fought and died for, hoping to link their own name to the story of eternity. She was all of desire, need and hunger, the pain that comes with pushing beyond all limits, with seeking out that which has never been seen, never been known before. She was the hurt that comes with seeing something perfect and so very lovely that you cannot bear to give it up, even though you can't keep it.

The sparrow at last grew brave enough to touch Her, a tiny stroke of beak across the smooth flesh of her half-open palm. A smile slowly crossed Her face and Her other fingers tWitched and closed even more tightly upon the shell and net. Her eyes opened at last, blue and milky grey as any newborn. But then they cleared and grew bright and brighter. They became blue and green, with dark and murky depths of black and violet beneath. She stretched and stirred, then rose to Her knees and to Her feet, golden hair cascading down. She swayed a moment or two, then stood up straight and faced the rising sun, looking into its white-gold heat with an unblinking gaze.

Her smile grew, betraying sharp white teeth, not quite those of a shark, but nearly so, and the golden net jangled like tiny bells as She tied it around her waist and turned from the sea to face the land. She raised one hand and the tiny sparrow jumped into the air and alighted there, black feet curled around one finger, his head cocked to peer intently into Her eyes. The dove flew up to settle on Her shoulder, soft feathers stroking Her neck.

Water filled her footprints as She began to walk upon the island that would soon house the first of Her many temples, salt-water like tears and like the sea. From the footprints grew tiny sprigs of myrtle, springing up until they had formed white flowers, the flowers giving way to black fruit, the wreath of the hopeful bride. She did not speak, not yet, but when She finally broke Her silence Her voice would be that of a nymph, a siren, an angel, a whore, a saint, a seductress and an innocent. She would charm and seduce even the Gods, so what chance anyone else?

The Golden Net

She who walks
She who knows well
The adoration of the sun
Men bend down
Their palms held low
Their heads bare
They kneel to beauty
And to the daughter of beauty
Pale feet passing
The jangle of gold
Her net brushes their backs
Her hair strokes over their skin
Ecstasy
Never before known
Never to know again
Pure and naked glory
They dare not raise their eyes
Lest they be burnt and scarred
She is night
And night's daughter
And brighter than any star
She needs no more praise than this
One whisper
One tender kiss
Placed upon Her open palm
A promise made
And set upon a heart
Laid bare by Her passing
By her scent
Her grace
Her touch

The waves rush in. The waves rush out, leaving treasures behind, bits of pearly shell, polished glass, driftwood fashioned into odd shapes, even tiny pieces of semi-precious stone. Amber may come from the depths of the sea, a gift from the ancient past, red and yellow, cognac and cream. Slippery tears of the sun and as representative of life as gold, it was likely amber which the Norse Goddess Freya bargained for from the cave-dwellers and wore as a symbol of the power of life and desire that She held over all. For amber is alive and a gift of both the land and of the sea.

Aphrodite is also a gift of the sea, a Goddess of the wonders to be found below the waters. Despite being known for the most part as the Greek Goddess of Love, She is also a deity of fertility, sailing, and, for the Spartans, a Goddess of war. Her name in Greek stems from the word *aphros*, which means foam and it's said that She Herself sprang up from sea foam. But then desire and the sea are linked, as can be seen in the fact that one of Aphrodite's symbols is the scalloped-edge seashell or *kteis* in Greek, a word also associated with female genitals. The famous painting by Botticelli, *The Birth of Venus*, shows Her standing within a giant version of such a shell on the morning of Her birth.

In the beginning, the four primal forces danced upon the Earth— the fires from deep below the ground emerging through volcanoes to destroy and to create, the great primeval ocean, the cauldron where life would someday be born, the rushing currents of the air, or what would someday be air, and the Earth Herself, vast continents strange and unfamiliar to us. Life sprang from the ground and from the sea, from where water and earth met and mingled. Life was sparked into existence by the fire of the sun, by light and love, the ultimate powers of the Divine Source. With breath then, with air, came spirit and so consciousness of self.

Like earth, water is one of the two elements required to create physical form. We are, in fact, made up of mostly water. Water flows into and through us like an ever-renewing spring. We are all creatures of the tidal forces, of our emotional currents, and we respond to them much as the sea does to the moon. In fact, being so much of the water, we are also deeply affected by the ebb and flow of the moon's gravity. Women bleed in tune with the changing face of the moon and we are all emotionally tied to Her power as much as to Mother Earth's, the full moon capable of driving us all just a little crazy sometimes.

There are two main stories of the birth of Aphrodite and both of them involve water. One is that She sprang up from the sea foam which came from the severed genitals of Uranus when they fell into the ocean during the massive war between the Titans and the upstart Gods of Mount Olympus. The other story is that She is the daughter of Zeus and Dione, who was Herself a child of Oceanus and Tethys, a water God and an earth Goddess. In some earlier myths, Dione was even the wife of Zeus before Hera arrived on the scene and She was quite possibly also the mother of Dionysus.

Whichever story you ascribe to, after Aphrodite came into being She was carried on a wave or in a scalloped shell to eventually settle on Cyprus, one of Her places of worship in ancient times. It's said that flowers and grass appeared as She walked on land for the very first time, perhaps one of the reasons why She was so well-loved by the Seasons, maidens who, like Dione, were considered the daughters of Thetys or Thetis, a creator goddess. If Aphrodite was, indeed, born of Dione, then the Seasons would have been Her "aunts."

Aphrodite's main animals are fish and birds, particularly doves and sparrows because the Greeks considered them to have an amorous nature. Unsurprisingly, the sea and seafood are still considered to have close associations with sex and seduction. The word *aphrodisiac*—which includes some seafood—is taken from the name of Aphrodite. Her priestesses of old had a ritual where they would bathe in the sea and thus be renewed and stay ever beautiful, desirable, and young just as their Goddess. They also wore nets in honor of the magickal golden net of Aphrodite, the net being another permutation of the web of Fate, the wheel of fortune, and the maze.

What does it mean then that the premiere Goddess of desire and beauty is said to be of the sea foam, that She is so closely linked to the sea? Among other things, it tells us that She is one of the living masks of the powers of the West, of the waves and of the waters. She is related to waters everywhere, from the bounty and majesty of the wide-flung seas, the deep dark pools which are gateways to other realms, the wells of promise and sacrifice—of which the Wishing Well descends—to the bowls of black water wherein visions can be seen, and the rivers which form boundaries and wellsprings of power.

These sorts of powers contain both light and dark aspects. Equally, despite Her strong association with love and beauty, Aphrodite isn't all sweetness and light either. She is the light which shines through a glass darkly, the rush of blood in passion and in fear, in rage and in desire. Some legends claim that She is the eldest of the Three Fates and even make Her sister to the Furies, those terrifying beings who punish oath breakers. Some of Her other ancient names translate to *the dark one*, a *slayer of men*, and Aphrodite *of the tombs*, which have definite overtones of a War Goddess.

But why would Aphrodite, a Goddess of love and fertility, also be considered a dark figure associated with tombs and with death? Well, for one thing, no God or Goddess is as one-sided as They are often portrayed today. It's merely our shorthand, or the shorthand of those who study mythology as outsiders, that lends itself to seeing the Gods as symbols or characters in a story and not as beings as complex as anyone you might meet and get to know. The Gods have personalities and Their worshippers form personal relationships with Them, learning from shared experience what They are like and forging a lasting bond as a result.

Just as we are not just one thing or another, all good or all bad, so the Gods are complex entities and can represent many qualities. These qualities may mesh well together or appear at times to conflict just as our own interests and beliefs and thoughts may not always mesh together smoothly. Of course, Aphrodite is not just love, but *passion*, all encompassing, all consuming. And when it comes to passion how can it be anything other than complex? How can it not have its bright and its dark side?

Aphrodite says: *"I was not so much born of the sea, but of desire. What is desire but a yearning, but a need too long denied. When the truth is that what you most desire you must seek, find it or find it not, and in the finding come to realize that your desire was never further than your heart's fondest wish away. What is that wish? What is that desire? Where does your heart most long to lead you? To another…oh, to another. Not to there find what you lost, but there to find what you desire, a mirror for your own light, your shadow, your lover's lover."*

Passion gives us the word *passionate*, but also the word *passive*. We tend to see passive as opposite to active, in which passive takes a submissive or non-active role. Yet, passive did not always mean a lack of action, of just taking things, even to the point of letting someone walk all over you. Passive once meant taking an active part in a different way. Being the passive party meant you were filled with passion and, more than that, you inspired the other party to action through the strength of your passion. As an example, the passion of a person seeking to plant trees or flowers in an otherwise rundown old park may inspire others to also take action and plant trees in other places in need of green, growing things. Or, when it comes to making love, the passive party is he or she who inspires their lover to be more fervent.

People are attracted to those who are passionate and it summons passion within them, either for the same object or idea or for something else that is dear to their hearts. Passion is transmittable, contagious even, and action is what results from this fire. Action

39

can take many forms, even as the passion which inspired it in the first place can take many forms. But though passion is full of creative fire, like all fires it may burn out of control. When it fills us up, spilling over into action, there remains the risk of it taking over our lives, even destroying us or those around us.

Aphrodite may be incredibly lovely, eminently desirable, and mother of inspiration, but She is pain as much pleasure, death as well as life. There is a fine line between passion and obsession, between fascination and fixation. Often, each shades the other. There's no help for it. True beauty, the beauty of the Gods and of the great powers of the universe, is also terrible, as in terrifying. The beauty of something so overwhelming, so incredible, that as much as we admire and adore it, it's also acutely painful to experience. Much as we want to continue to be there, to feel it, to see it, we cannot bear the touch of it for long, even though afterwards we are drawn to seek it out again and again. Inspiration and the beauty of the Gods is like that and we can become addicted to it like the poets of old, reaching for the unreachable.

But what exactly is inspiration? Inspiration is what makes us want to create and to change things. It can be described as a power, an urge, as encouragement, or as a feeling welling up deep inside us until we have to find a way to channel it into being. In other words, what inspires is what gets us out of bed in the morning, not with a grumble, but with a smile, with excitement. It's what we chase after and what we most desire and nothing else matters then, not hunger or thirst or making it to that appointment or to work or even spending time with our loved ones.

We have to ask then—what is it that we desire? Do we give in to it or do we turn away, afraid of what others might think, telling ourselves that we have duties to fulfill and more important appointments to keep. Do we follow our hearts or do we lock them away in a box and hide the key, even from ourselves. Do we allow ourselves to chase after false gems, the many sparkling things that demand that we notice them, that tell us that they will feed our need, only to prove false in the end, nothing but paste and glass. When what we really need is that one thing, the one worth all the others, and the only thing worth giving up everything for. We can't really do powerful magick to get what we want without bringing desire into it, the requisite emotional fire.

Do you want to feel really alive? Do you long to see the world as a child once again, with that excitement of discovery of all its bright colors, sounds, textures, tastes, all those incredible sensations we missed when we were in the land of the dead, unable to taste and to touch. What can make that real, make that happen again, if not by restoring our passion for the world. When we do, we can also find our inspiration for passion and inspiration go hand in hand. We are passionate about what inspires us and what inspires us makes us passionate. Together, they make us live again, to remember what life can and should be.

Our senses can become dulled and dim and go to sleep because we are bored with our lives, exhausted by what's become routine. We fear living a life without meaning, without hope, but that's also what we begin to believe is the only thing out there. We search and search for meaning, for a way to come alive again, but are steered off on wild goosechase after wild goosechase, as society tells us that what we need are *things* in order to be happy and fulfilled. A new car, a new pair of shoes, a boat, a vacation, a bigger and better television, the list is endless. All of which may make us feel good for a little while, but only a little while. It never lasts.

Sometimes, it's not dullness alone which turns us off to the world, but stress as well, that constant companion of modern life. We just can't handle any more and so we shut down, tune out, dull our emotions and perceptions. Eventually, living a monochromatic life becomes a habit, making it all the more difficult to break out of the routine and rouse our senses once more, reconnecting to the blinding beauty of the greater world still going on all around us. We may even begin to fear the expansion of our senses, our own feelings, afraid that we no longer know how to handle them. We become afraid that if we re-open that door it will all come rushing out of us, a mad torrent that might destroy everything in its path. We call this dull world the normal world, deciding that those moments of expansion are just oddities, something that either marks us as insane or exalted.

It doesn't help that modern society often aims to *keep* us muted or forces us to channel our emotions only in the ways it desires. Of course, society needs rules in order to function, but rules can sometimes go too far, become restrictive, or too much in favor of those who make the rules. It's harder to control those who are in touch with their emotions, who use it to effect change in the world. So, instead we are taught to erect walls between us and not build so many bridges. We are taught to be uncomfortable when people display their emotions in public or in ways which don't play by the spoken or unspoken rules. We are taught not to be Witches, not to be cunning folk, not to be in touch with our hearts and our power.

Far better to allow our emotions to flow naturally, to gain practice in channeling them correctly, so that we can feel confident that they won't end up someday overwhelming us. In this way, emotion is a lot like magick—we need practice to master both. Experience is the best and most lasting teacher in this regard. Good experiences and bad experiences both teach us as they also create memories in conjunction with the feelings that accompany them. Change your feelings and you can change how you think and how you act. Change these and you change the world you live in. Harness your emotions and fix them to intention and you have a powerful well to call upon in all your pursuits, common or Otherworldly.

This passion makes us feel alive and this passion can be used as a tool in the Arts, especially the Art of magick. When we get back in touch with our feelings and our passion, we can use that to further all that we do, including spells and ritual. Not only are other people drawn to us by the power of our passions, but non-human entities begin to notice our flame, a brilliant light that lures them near. Passion not only makes us more powerful, but it also attracts powerful allies to us. Forging this passion into a tool benefits our artistic and magickal goals. It can also aid in creating a bridge to the Otherworld, both to travel there and to succeed in returning again. You have to feel where you are going, where you long and desire to go, and you must feel your way home to where you belong, to where your blood lies buried.

If we allow the river to flow through us rather than being dammed up—the river of our emotions, our abilities, our talents, and the natural power that springs not just from our physical bodies but our spirits—we can accomplish great things. When we allow ourselves to feel truly alive, we forge a connection to our spirits. We can not only make a bridge, but become a bridge between the separate aspects of our own inner selves. Our spirits can traverse this bridge as other spirits can travel from Faery to this world.

Aphrodite tells us that *"If you dance within your own footsteps, you dance within. The journey you go on takes you deep. What springs from your steps comes from within, from the source deep inside you. It is a summoning, but who knows what or why? That is the real question, though the only way to answer it is to dance."*

Many other doors will open when we open that inner door to our emotional strengths. We can learn how to put that expanded power to good use, as over time and with practice, we learn how to channel greater and greater powers, powers that would be dangerous to otherwise allow through us without that experience. Not just the energies of creation and passion and inspiration, but powers that few of us can even imagine at the present time, including some that have no name, no words in English, capable of describing them.

43

Aphrodite's passion flows like water, the deep currents of tide and of flood. Nothing can stop water once it decides to go somewhere. Water can wear away solid stone, entire mountains. It can make deserts bloom. Water is life. Water flows as our emotions flow, so that it's no coincidence that when that flow is constricted or stopped that we can grow ill. We block up not just the free and natural and healthy currents of emotion and energy inside us, but we can become debris blocking the wider flow of energy in the world we all live in. Part of the job of the cunning folk, of Witches, is to make sure that the currents flow and, to do that, we need to have our own currents in good working order. The energy lines and nodes of the land reflect those that lie within.

Feelings are powerful. We all know that. One reason is that how we feel informs what we believe and how we believe affects how we see the world; we can only see the world through the lenses we bring, through the filters we have created, and to change the world we need to change those filters. To see past our filters is one of the goals of a spiritual life, of the occult path. It's walking in the footsteps of Aphrodite, leaving flowers and green grass behind. It's learning to see what is really going on, both out there and inside us and to know how each reflects and affects the other, to understand the mystery of the moon and the sun.

If we desire to have a direct experience of the Divine, to have our lives touched by something as profoundly beautiful as it is frightening, it all begins within. It starts with the rediscovery of our innate passion. It involves no longer tuning out, but tuning in—renewing our connection with the frequency of life we have all but forgotten about and that some of us have even been trained to fear and to avoid. It involves renewing our ability to see this world and other worlds, for how can we go beyond this world if we can't first see behind the mask? We don't even pay all that much attention sometimes to our five ordinary senses, so how can we seek to see in an extraordinary fashion?

One way of achieving a trance state is by shutting out all distractions, shutting down sensory input, but what Aphrodite can show is another path to the same end. Instead of tuning out we can tune in and concentrate all our senses on the world around us, trying to take it all in. We choose to shut out the filter rather than the world and set our senses to flying, seeing where they can take us. To be honest, it's difficult enough to see the Otherworld, let alone when we haven't learned how to first see our own. And if we can't see the Otherworld, we can't go there.

It's no coincidence that doves were once used for sacrifices as they were considered to be travelers between this world and the Other. As funerary birds, doves often symbolized the souls of the dead and their cousins, pigeons, have been used to carry messages all the way back to the time of ancient Rome. The dove is one of Aphrodite's birds, as well as being sacred to Her lover, Adonis. Doves also belong to the God of wine, Bacchus, the Roman Dionysus.

Doves were associated with Astarte and Ishtar, while in Christian mythology they are an image of the Holy Spirit. But then the Holy Spirit was always meant to be the female aspect of the Trinity, the missing "mother" figure to balance out the Father and the Child. Sometimes, the dove was shown with a star, which perhaps shows a link to the many Goddesses who claim the title of Queen of Heaven, including the Virgin Mary. Along those lines, doves symbolize purity, peace, and innocence, but what has been overlooked in recent times is that they also have long represented love and voluptuousness.

The other bird sacred to Aphrodite was the lowly sparrow. Sparrows represent the commonplace, the ordinary, what seems small and insignificant. Hence the old adage that God is aware of everything because He is aware of each and every sparrow and every sparrow's fall. Sparrows were also associated with lust and lewd impulses, with wanton desire, the same revelry linked to Dionysus and our old friend, Bacchus. Whereas the dove has long been one of the ways to carry messages to the Divine, to lift prayers to the heavens, the sparrow represents common life. One represents spiritual or Divine love and the other its more earthly aspect.

The real Aphrodite is certainly a cross between the spiritual dove and the secular sparrow, between agape and sex. She is a Goddess of a hunger both spiritual and physical, of necessity, of a longing for something more, an experience of bliss. Science talks about this force of attraction, of one thing being drawn by natural law to another, though they would probably not like to admit that the same power which works on planets and stars also works between two people. But it's essentially the same force, a force that Witches have long acknowledged and used to their advantage since they know and understand how like attracts like, how a reflection forms a connection between two things.

It can be said this reflective nature is caused by the duality of time. In Eternity, all things are one thing, but once you exist in time, opposites come into existence. All sorts of opposites, from the forces of action and reaction, up and down, light and dark, real and unreal, seen and unseen, revealed and hidden, the list is endless. When so-called opposites are drawn to each other it's because they were once truly one thing and, when and if they do come back together, they do so in memory of the original whole. They are drawn together to reflect the Source which first gave birth to them. They are drawn together by a force and a power that cannot be denied.

But what is this power, this force? Simply put, it is Love. Science likes to call it gravity, but the spiritual component of gravity is Love and Love is what lies behind the law of attraction. Gravity is just the outward appearance, the action and reaction, not the totality, not the real reason why planets and moons spin towards and away from each other, not the real reason we are drawn towards the Earth.

46

Aphrodite is one of the masks that represent this great power of mutual attraction. She is the mad passion that lies behind the force of attraction, one of the primary powers of the universe. Passion is what helps bind the entire universe together, not just one single person to another, not just one single particle to another. Carbon is so successful an element, because it's very good at binding with many other elements, thus making all sorts of new things. Basically, it desires other elements and other elements desire it.

Another name for such magickal attraction might be called *charm*. Certain people we meet are considered to be charming, or in other words, they are somehow capable of attracting others to them and to their ideas, of getting them to do what they want, and generally being fascinating to anyone who bumps into them. In a way, charming people share many of the same attributes as the element of carbon.

It's also no coincidence that the word charm means a chant, poem, spell, or an item charged with magickal virtues or properties. Generally, charms are meant to bring something to us or to avert something from us, action and reaction again. Chants and spells are often used for much the same purpose, allowing us to attract everything from a lover to money to good health to luck, whatever we need and desire. They also allow us to repel ill luck or illness.

But what is it that we desire? We need to know that before we can start focusing our intent, let alone pour energy into it. One way of figuring that out is by seeing what we desire, what interests us, what fascinates us. Sure, sometimes we simply desire what we require, such as a roof over our heads, food on the table, a job, a car, and so on. But that's a spell for need, and often we want more than that. So what is fascination then, if what we are drawn towards is said to have captured our attention, to have charmed us, so we are madly attracted to it.

We pour bits of ourselves into what attracts us. We pour our emotions into it. Emotions are one of the key components of doing magick for when we focus emotional energy on something or someone we are feeding the spell as well as proving a link to what it is the spell is aimed at. We become linked together, just as a link is created between ourselves and what fascinates us. What sparks our emotions gives us clues to discovering our desires and, once we know that, we can consciously pour energy and intent into those desires.

Aphrodite tells us "*Fascination is a snare, feathered, furred, vibrant, perfumed. We may know it is a snare, yet we cannot escape it for it is our own desire which traps us. We don't seek to escape for we long for the trap, the pleasure. We feel and that is the pull, the draw, the sweet seduction. The priestess and the whore know much the same secrets, though the expression is different.*"

To call upon Aphrodite is to call upon passion, emotion, and a love that is both earthly and spiritual. It's part of hooking into the connective forces of the universe, a way of understanding those connective forces that can lead to being able to attract what you need into your life. Fascination is one of the old powers of Witches and cunning folk of all kinds. We use passion to active and feed our spells and charms, calling what we desire to us or to those who come to us for aid or advice.

Aphrodite is the daughter of passion, illuminating and blinding. We can, through Her, act as both the sparrow and the dove, experiencing a secular and a divine love, and awaken not just to the ordinary world, but to the myriads of supernatural ones, as well. We can learn how to recognize and use the strength of our passions to do magick and visit those other worlds. Just as we can charm our way into the regard of others, be they of a mortal or Divine nature.

Awakening

Words etch razors and claws
Dark blood welling up
Spilling over to pearl
Poetry burned deep into the page
Talons clutching sharp
Framing shoulders bent to the praise
Fragrant wings caressing
Each feather a thought
Dreams in the eyes of a dove
The sparrow's talk
Nest eggs gathered blue and golden
Not a bird but a serpent
Sea and fire and salt
Green poison the wine of desire
In an amethyst cup
Don't drink unless you want the hurt
Don't scream
This is what you asked for
Down on the unquiet shores
With a whispered spell
A sprinkling of shells
Shark's teeth
Rose petals crushed to breath
And gone

It's almost too easy to fall asleep and no longer really notice the world around us, the passage of each separate moment. Concentrating on the past or on the future too much negates the moment we are in right here, right now. The past and the future are aspects of time, rippling out in opposite directions from the eternal now. In order to slip into that other world we must step into the space between time, between the passage of the moments. We must stretch them out until time slows to a standstill and the universe expands, providing understandings not possible while caught up in time, understandings often paradoxical while in time. It's an experience not easily translatable into words, especially since most languages are so rooted in time, particularly linear time. But the experience can be carried in our blood and feelings, if not retained in our minds.

But then, experiences are all we can really have in life, all that is truly ours. Possessions, despite being physical, material objects, are what are really *immaterial.* They are shadows, far more fleeting than experiences, and we eventually lose them. While who and what we truly are at the core can never be lost. No one and nothing can destroy a spirit and we are all spirits. No one and nothing but that spirit itself, can stop it from being.

One reason why we are here is to have experiences. They are meant to teach us, to transform us and become a part of us, incorporated into our lives. Experiences become a part of our own energies, or they can help clear away what doesn't belong in our energies. Over time, we change and yet we don't really change, for what changes is only that which needs to; our core self remains constant, the still point around which everything else spins. That is what we must always hold onto, even as the world transforms around us.

At the same time, though, we need to figure out how to rid ourselves of experiences that become attached to us and which do *not* empower. These experiences are not truly a part of us nor should they be. They can block our path rather than impelling us forward on it. Sometimes, these energies have been imparted to us by others, whether by individuals or society, either to control us or as a projection of their own limitations and fears that have latched onto us. Sometimes, even those who are basically well meaning can instill energies into us that are not really to our benefit. The more open we are, the higher the risk of something like this happening, which explains in part why we carry so many issues from our childhood.

50

When it comes to those who *do* mean us harm, the emotions of hurt and anger and fear and doubt and shame can be aimed at us by them, consciously or unconsciously, attempting to fool us into believing they're part of us, part of our own issues. This is an aspect of negative magick and it's almost like a disease. These kinds of energies can even, over time, gain a life and a sentience almost of their own and become something akin to a conscious virus passing from one person to the next, one generation to the next. Growing the whole time in power, cunning and intensity, until at last someone stands up and breaks their hold, taking back the power that has fed them.

Of course, most of us don't run into those kinds of energies very often, thank goodness, but we all have our own energies and entities unnatural to us that need to be purged from our system and the damage they've caused allowed at last to heal. This is important since they can harm not just us but also project into our physical bodies and cause sickness. They can broadcast outward from us and harm others, as well, whether we are aware of it or not. Greed is one such spiritual virus, as is multi-generational child abuse; they become living entities over time and have a will to survive, no matter the cost.

One way to purge ourselves and promote healing lies in filling ourselves with beauty, with hope, joy and pleasure. The more joy and happiness we can feel, the better and healthier we will be both mentally and physically. The stronger the joy we allow to infuse us as deeply and as often as possible, the more powerful and lasting its effects will be. What we build from this joy also can become conscious and aware and have an influence above and beyond the sphere of our own lives. It's almost a living ecstasy, one that we can pass to others if they desire it and that we can use to charm or charge spells and objects.

Like attracts like. We see what is beautiful—more than that, we *experience* beauty—and as it elevates us, our bodies and feelings are elevated. The more we can feel what is good and right, the more good and right will come into our lives. The more often we experience true happiness, the easier it will come. Like a road much taken and well loved, it will become a way we know almost instinctively and can always remember, even when life turns difficult. Sure, that may sound simplistic on the surface, but it's not really that easy. We can't wish really hard, work all that positive thinking jazz, and have everything just drop into our laps. It takes time and it takes effort to transform our inner landscape and it can be a painful, scary process. But the ecstasy of divine beauty and joy can prove a necessary tool in that regard.

Of course, beauty and inspiration may be found in high and rugged mountains, in serene lakes, in forests of soaring trees, in a rainbow arching up from a misty waterfall; it's easy to see the mystery of the Divine in such scenes and be moved by them. Even the ocean of the Muse is entrancing with all its dangers and the secrets inherent in deep waters. It's natural to see beauty in that which is wild and grand and majestic, yet beauty also resides in the smallest of things and in the strangest of places. As Witches and cunning ones, we have to see what the majority do not, to see with the eye of an artist. Through learning how to see, really see, we can then turn the smaller wheels which are a part of the greater wheels.

Yet beauty, great or small, is but the means of visible expression of powers that are grander still, that are so beautiful and dangerous and mysterious that to grasp them can cause not just emotional and mental, but actual physical pain. The material world as we know it is a projection of forces that can't easily be seen or known. Yet, through the Arts, we can learn to see more, because the power of the Muse opens us up to experience. We find depths within us and all around us and in exploration of those depths, learn to see all over again. What awaits is the larger universe, the divine Beingness that is infinitely complex and yet strangely simple. We may yet learn to walk upon the shores of Aphrodite, following Her footsteps into the dawn.

True perception comes with a price, though. Not only can it prove difficult to obtain, but it's even more difficult to hold onto. Physically, we are not really made to handle all that *everythingness* all at once. Certainly, if that intense level of perception is turned on and we can't figure out how to shut it off again we could find it hard to live anything approaching a "normal" life.

Face it, most of us are not cut out to be saints or gurus, which isn't to say that we don't need saints or gurus, but the society we live in must support their existence and the Western world just isn't generally set up to do that. This doesn't mean that we can't pursue this sort of divine perception or that it's of no use. As Witches, we have to learn how to open that door—and close it again at will—which is all part of claiming the supernatural vision of Faery, the Second Sight, not just to be able to see into the Otherworld, but deeper into this world, as well.

Aphrodite asks us to *"look, look, look…what do you see? Is the world plain? Is it boring? Is it sad? The world is, but perception remains yours to choose. Why then, do so many choose a sad world, a boring one, unbeautiful and without lasting joy or hope? Why do they choose such a world unless they believe there can be no other, and who has taught them that, save those who profit from such a sad world.*

Think well upon this. Where lies the benefit to such a thing, and who benefits from it? There, you will find the creators of the sad world, the hard one, the one so many mislike. Will you let them keep you locked away forever from life, from truth, from beauty, from the strength of your own hearts?

Make your own world—do not let it be made for you."

Aphrodite represents an unchained and unfettered life. She is the beauty of life encompassing joy and pain in full measure. She is that missing passion we long for, that electrifying spark which makes us feel awake and aware. She is the beauty that wakes us up, overwhelming and shocking, and She is the passion that keeps us awake afterwards. We hunger for what She has to offer us, yet we fear it at the same time. We fear to feel, to turn that awareness back on. It can just hurt too much.

We want beauty. We want passion. We want to be glad in who we are and what we are doing, for nothing else really lasts. Material objects, no matter how nice, are substitutes for the real thing and we tend to call that real thing *happiness*. But as no two people will find happiness in quite the same way—even though the source of lasting happiness and fulfillment always comes from within—beauty comes at people in different ways. Everyone experiences the Goddess of Passion for themselves, seeing Her through their own shade and flavor of desire. We all have our beauties and our passions, no matter what shape they take. We can all be touched, moved, roused, and our composure shattered by what we see and experience, allowing the greater world to come rushing back in.

The Divine asks that we wake up and be aware. The Muse begs us to open up our senses, all of our senses, even the ethereal ones, and let the world in. She asks us to see and to live as we are meant to see and to live, to live our purpose that is our true being. For we when we stop being aware then we risk losing ourselves and shutting out the greater world. Of course, it's immensely difficult to exist like that all the time. It's kind of like going around with all of your skin off. Living with full awareness is just too much to take in on a daily basis and our instinctual reaction is to shut down, to withdraw, and put the world back behind a protective screen.

The problem is, though, that most of us have already done that. We fell asleep a long time ago and share a dream we name reality. Still, in the past, there were certain ways, certain teachings that could help go beyond the dream, to wake up and to remember. And, luckily, there remain rituals and magicks that can help open our eyes to worlds beyond and what moves behind the surface of things, of this "place" called reality. We just have to find which ones work for us, practicing them until they release their power and insight and release us.

Ritual is meant to transform, to transcend and transport one to other worlds and states of existence. It's not an end unto itself, merely celebration, but a tool to touch that which can't otherwise be touched, and part of that has to do with opening one's self up to passion. Ritual should be passionate. It should be pleasurable, beautiful, exalted, and rooted in the physical senses all at the same time. It should involve exploration and risk and contact with the Divine, otherwise what are you doing?

For true beauty has darkness to it as much as light and we risk the dark each time we pursue the light. We need what the fertile dark can give us, but it also contains dread gifts and challenges. It can overwhelm us if we're not ready. Still, we must consume the gift of the Muse whole and entire, no half-measures, and be consumed by it in turn. We have to. Otherwise, we haven't really opened the door. Otherwise, we may still be asleep.

As Aphrodite says "*I am the blossom as well as the wilted bloom. The dried husk and the petal wet with dew. I am both rose and thorn, pain and pleasure, fear and adoration, the mask as well as what the mask conceals.*

I come from life and death for I was born from that which nurtures both and though no shore yet retains my mark, the imprint of my step, yet all the world knows me full well. My mark is in their veins and my footprints raise armies and command love and hate, loyalty beyond death, and enmity that is all consuming and as grand a passion as any other more respectable one.

Who am I? You know me. You all know me. I am that which makes this life worth the living of it and I am that which makes death not an enemy to be defeated, but a lover to be courted. Who am I? Answer that and you begin to know who you are."

Aphrodite is a Goddess of awakenings, uncanny, catastrophic, illuminating and terrifying. Which makes it all the more sad that She should have been relegated in today's world to being a Goddess of romance, sweet and pretty, sure, but not much good for anything else except the occasional love spell. When the awful truth is that Aphrodite is a Goddess of undeniable passion; passion that binds the universe together into a web of mutual need, and mutual attraction. The web that is Fate and finds its echo in Aphrodite's golden net, in Her role as one of the spinners, continually creating connections and reflections.

It does little good to open to the Otherworld if we don't have a firm grounding in this one. We must love this place enough to really see it and wish to make it all the more lovely by what we can bring to it. The greatest gift that of being who we are and experiencing that to the absolute fullest. We can't find magick in other places if we can't find it in ourselves, as we can't see beauty unless we can see it in ourselves.

A Prayer to Aphrodite

Aphrodite
Glorious one
Shimmering and perfect
The living pearl of the sea
You who were born of death
And of the trembling dawn
You who walk upon the shore
Of memory
Which encompasses all
Hope and loss
Dream and desire
True beauty to eclipse
Even the dance of the planets
The schemes of both
Gods and man
All that passes away
Give to me
The salt and the sweet
Dust and honey
Milk and wine
And the life which springs forth
From blushing promise
And the painful thorn
Of that which cannot last
Pierce my heart
And let me see
The world as it is
As it was ever meant to be.

Rite to Ask a Vision of Aphrodite

You might want to acquire some sea salt for this ritual. Using a blue or a blue-green glass bowl to hold the saltwater would also be a nice touch. For the altar, use a black or dark blue altar cloth or a patterned cloth with waves or sea animals or fish. Anything that reminds you of the sea is appropriate, even if the only link having acquired it at some sea-side shop. The association is what matters.

A golden net can be painted on the cloth or a small net-like golden scarf, piece of lace, or even a painted doily can be used. When you are not using it in ritual, you might keep the golden net next to a statue of Aphrodite, perhaps even wrapped around Her hips.

Position the glass bowl in the center of the altar. The edge of the net can be decorated with shells or they can be placed around the base of the bowl.

Cast the circle in whatever manner you choose.

Remove all the items from the altar except for the bowl that contains the salt water. If it is your custom to bless water and salt, then it should be blessed by this time. You may also take your salt-water and add more salt to it until it is akin to seawater.

Kneel next to the altar if possible and put both your hands over the bowl, palm downwards. If you are working in a group, the Priestess or the Priest or both together may hold out their hands over the bowl. The words can be said by them or everyone in the circle can say it together or take it in parts. If you like, everyone may hold their hands, palms inwards, towards the bowl at the center of the circle.

Make of this bowl
The rim of the horizon
That we may see beyond the mask
Below the waves
To what desire dreams
And what the web entangles
Born of the great oceans
Of sea and of sky
Of the farthest unknown shores
Wherein the stars
Tell the tale
Of gods and of monsters
Let us dream true
Let us see clear
And come to walk upon the edge
Between what is
What was
And what may yet come to be

If the bowl cannot be easily seen from its place on the altar, remove it and set it in the center of the group—moving the altar to the North if you need extra space. The bowl should be set where everyone see into it without too much trouble. The black or dark blue cloth and golden net can be kept beneath the bowl.

A chosen person or the Priest/Priestess at this point invokes the Goddess, saying:

We invoke
And call upon your power
Aphrodite
Give us visions
Grant us dreams
Show us the beauty of this world
Of all the worlds
Even those that lie hidden

Within the circle
Of our own hearts

We are not afraid
Show us oh siren
The song of our souls
The songs as yet unsung
And unknown
But which need to be known
Which need to be sung
Grace us with gifts
Of your poetry and praise
All that is meant
To awaken joy

You or all may whisper then, repeating:

Show us
Show us
We are not afraid
Aphrodite
Aphrodite
Aphrodite

Continue to whisper these words as you stare into the bowl of salt water until a vision comes. Your eyes can close in the process. Your voice may also grow softer and softer, slower and slower, until it ceases altogether. Imagine if you will that the sound you have created has merged with the sound of waves. In fact, if you find it difficult to just let go and drift, it may be helpful to have ocean sounds playing somewhere in the background.

You might want to imagine the bowl of saltwater as though it's a doorway to the sea, picturing yourself stepping through it and plunging into the waters. Or envision it expanding larger and larger until you can feel and see and smell the ocean all around you.

If you find this difficult, you might want to add words to the ritual to that effect, helping to guide you to where you want to go.

If a vision does not come this first time, try again, for with practice and intent and invocation of the Goddess, much may be seen. Also, the word vision is often misleading because visions may take the form of sounds or sensations, feelings or even smells. Follow any feeling or odd sensation down into the depths, allowing the currents to carry you where you need to go

If you wish to try to share a dream with a group you are working with, everyone in the circle can hold hands as they stare into the bowl, softly whispering and/or focusing on what you wish to explore, where you want to go, what you need to know. You may not have exactly the same experience, especially at first, but depending on the strength of your bonds and how long you have worked together, quite often you will see something similar, find a commonality.

Never forget to thank the Goddess for Her gifts, for Her visions or for any words, songs, and other works of Art which come into being as a result of this ritual.

Blessing Rite of Aphrodite

Cast your circle as usual.

Take a shell or a bowl where you normally mix salt and water and use enough salt to approximate seawater.

Have each person who wishes to ask Aphrodite's blessing come forward one at a time to stand before the Priestess of the ritual. The Priestess may lightly touch each person with some of the saltwater, once right above the genitals (midway to the navel), once over the heart, over each closed eyelid, and at last upon the brow.

The Priestess says:

> **May the blessings of Aphrodite**
> **Queen of living desire**
> **Be upon you**
> **Let your eyes be opened**
> **To the world**
> **Let your heart grow light**
> **May you speak of all**
> **That is most beautiful**
> **And most terrible**
> **Strange and familiar**
> **Of life and death**
> **Of love and delight**
> **And of the joys**
> **To be found in the body**
> **The door to bliss**
> **And to knowledge of the eternal**
> **By the star of the sea**
> **Be awakened**
> **Be joyful**
> **Be free**

Once all have been marked with the saltwater, invoke Aphrodite into the Priestess. Everyone may at that point take turns coming before Her and asking what they would, whether advice or blessings. Remember, that if you are asking for a favor then something needs to be offered in return.

This offering can take the form of a service or a gift that She would like, especially something that stems from your own creativity. For example, writing a poem about the Muse and posting it online, creating a ritual of your own and leading it, or making a wreath of flowers and other biodegradable material and setting it adrift on a local river. Giving these kinds of gifts to the waters is one good way of getting them to the Muse.

You can then dismiss Her or ask Her to first bless and share any food or drink with you for the feast.

Feast of Aphrodite

Lay out a cloth on the altar or in the middle of the floor. Place a candleholder in the middle of the cloth, preferably with a white, pink, or ivory candle. If you have a statue of Aphrodite, set Her next to the candle, as well as fresh flowers or flower petals or a flowering plant if one is available. Again, pink or white or ivory flowers are best. A seashell or a string of pearls can be set next to the candle or at the feet of the statue. They can be the same shells or pearls that you might normally keep with the statue of the Goddess.

Set a bowl for libations before the statue or the candle. It can be ringed by flowers or by another necklace of pearl or shells. If you don't have a bowl that you regularly use for libations to the Gods, then any bowl will do. The bowl doesn't have to be large, but it shouldn't be too small, because you will be putting food and drink into it.

Every person attending the ritual should bring an item of food, enough for everyone in the circle to have a taste, plus two "extras." It doesn't have to be very big portions. In fact, it's probably better if they are smaller. Food that you have made yourself is a nice touch as well as food that you have spent some time arranging how it's presented on the plate or in the bowl. Finger food is actually best because it doesn't require a fork or spoon to eat or to serve.

As a note, rose petals are edible and can be obtained from some grocery stores or stores that cater to the creation of cakes or sweets. You shouldn't use rose petals from your own garden or elsewhere unless you're sure that they haven't been sprayed. Apples are, of course, also associated with Aphrodite, especially "golden" ones. Obviously, seafood of any kind is linked to the Goddess, though you might need to keep the food on ice in some fashion, just to be safe.

Everyone should have a own goblet or glass. What you pick to drink can be wine, red or pink preferably, but you can choose juice instead. In any case, it would be better for everyone to have a share of the same drink—whatever type you choose—rather than many different ones. A nice light apple cider or a sparkling apple juice would also work.

Cast a circle as you normally would.

Light the central candle, saying:

> **Gracious Goddess**
> **Queen of passion and of desire**
> **Of the breathless ebb**
> **And flow of the sea**
> **Of the hunger that burns**
> **In the hearts of man**
> **For love**
> **For life**
> **For something more**
> **Hear us**
> **See us**
> **We stand upon the shore**

Everyone takes a turn setting the small plate of food they have brought on the cloth surrounding the statue or the lit candle. You might also bow or courtesy at this time. The goblets or glasses can be set down in a ring around the edge of the cloth.

When done, all should join hands and the Priest or Priestess or a chosen person says:

> **Aphrodite**
> **Heed our call**
> **Bless this feast**
> **The touch**

The taste
The scent
A vision of bounty
And of beauty
Given to us
By the generosity of the earth
Of the seas
And by the sacrifice
Made pure and whole

If Aphrodite chooses to, She may show up at this time to bless the feast personally. You may also decide to deliberately invoke Her by focusing on a chosen Priestess and adding the words:

Aphrodite
We call upon thee
We invoke thee
Be welcome to our circle
To our feast
To our hearts

Otherwise, proceed to:

As we are given to
So we must also give
The way of the circle
The way of the sea
The way of the earth
Of all that lives and dies
Only to live once again

Each person takes turns picking up the plate they have brought, putting an item of food into the libation bowl. If you have invoked the Goddess into the ritual, you should offer the first item of food to Her directly. You may offer the piece of food to Her with a bow or curtsey and whatever words you desire. A simple "for you" is often good enough, though if you wish to speak more poetically it wouldn't go amiss.

After the libation or gift to the Goddess, each person eats a piece of food and hands the plate to the next person in the circle. As each person picks up their plate and libates a piece they may say:

> **One for each**
> **One for the all**
> **The first fruits and the last**
> **Bind us together**
> **We are the circle**

When the plate returns with a single piece remaining, the person who provided that food libates the final piece.

When you eat a piece of the feast from each of the plates, you should take your time and try to savor the taste, texture, and smell of what you're eating. You should concentrate not just on this, but on where the food came from—the plants, the animals, the earth, the sea—and try to remember that by eating this food you are taking part in a larger cycle, an intimate part of life and of death.

When the food is all gone, you can pick up your goblet and hold it out before you, towards the center of the circle. Pour or have someone pour wine or fruit juice into the goblets. If the Goddess is there, Her goblet should be filled first.

Take turns pouring a libation from your own cup, saying:

> **One for each**
> **One for the all**
> **The first drop and the last**
> **Bind us together**
> **We are the circle**

All should drink, taking the time to savor the taste and smell of the wine or juice, the effort that went into making it and the life that was given up. A small portion should remain in each cup in the end, enough to make a last libation. When the goblets are empty, they can be placed in the now empty plates and bowls.

Sit in the circle and hold hands, saying:

> **We are the sacrifice**
> **We are the feast**
> **The circle binds us together**
> **For we shall ever know love**

At this point, Aphrodite may be moved to join the circle and to speak through someone. Of course, if She is already there, this may be a good time to ask any questions of Her or simply get to know Her better. At the end of the rite, you can then ask Her politely to leave, or dismiss Her with a kiss.

Gifts of Aphrodite Ritual

For this ritual you might want to make a crown of pearls or shells. You could also make a golden net, one with shells attached to it. You can sometimes obtain real shells at antique stores or craft stores that carry gifts made out of natural items.

You can make a golden net large enough for a person to wear by taking a white or cream colored piece of netting or an open work shawl and painting it with gold paint. Of course, you might simply be able to find a shawl that is primarily gold-colored. You can also put gold colored sequins or rhinestones on it to give it even more glitter, along with small shells.

Cast a circle as usual.

Before starting the ritual, or directly after you have cast the circle, put on jewelry or other items that remind you of your life, of all that you do, both good and bad. You can also paint symbols on your skin, or do a combination of both. The symbols should represent your friends, your family, your hobbies, your work, everything that marks out the boundaries of your current life. For example, if you're a writer you could pin a pen or quill-shaped broach to your robe or paint one on your skin. If you work answering phones, you can paint the image of a phone or even clip your cell phone to your robe (turned off, of course).

Once everyone has put on the emblems of their current life and relationships, have the Priest or a chosen person say:

> **Like the Gods**
> **We have many masks**
> **Unlike the Gods**
> **Not all of ours are true**
> **Others may not see us**

As we really are
And we may not see ourselves
Our light and our lives
Can become obscured
And confused
For to see the world
Is to see ourselves
And to see ourselves
Is to see the world

The Priest then places a crown of pearls and shells on the head of the Priestess or a shell or pearl necklace around her neck. A large shell may also be handed to her or a gold colored net tied around her hips, saying:

Aphrodite
Priestess and Queen
Of the salt bitterness of the sea
And the bounty
Of golden honey
Lady of hope and desire
Of love and despair
Hear us
Answer our plea
Come to us
Upon fragrant smoke
Upon wings of terrible light
Quick and sure
Answer to our need
You who are beauty
And beauty's chain
You who are the song
And the voice to sing it
Aphrodite
Enter into your priestess (name)
Who awaits thy presence

One by one, each person in the circle should come before the Goddess and deliberately remove the items they have pinned to their robes. There should be a box or basket ready to collect the items. If you have painted symbols on your skin, have water and a cloth to wash off the symbols.

If the group is comfortable with practicing skyclad, you may all choose to remove your robes at this point. Otherwise, everyone can wear a short mostly transparent piece of cloth over their heads and remove it at this point. The thought is to stand as naked before the Goddess as possible.

The Goddess hands each person a seed or a tiny crystal stone or bead, saying:

> **Beauty is strength**
> **And strength, beauty**

She offers them a drink from Her cup, saying:

> **All by and to and for**
> **The greatest power of all**
> **Which is love**

Each person responds by telling the Goddess and the rest of those in the circle the length of time they are pledging to this task, be it a month or three months, a year and a day or even longer. The seed or bead or crystal represents the kernel from which they have sworn to bring something into the world.

When all have come before the Goddess and taken a drink and received the crystal or seed or bead, the Priest says:

> **It is by our will**
> **That these seeds shall grow**
> **It is by our choice**

73

That what grows
Shall take shape
They shall not fall on
Fallow ground
So we swear
By the gift of the goddess
And by the promises
We have already made

All respond:

So sworn
So mote it be
The seed lies within
I shall not turn aside
From the task

Each person takes the seed or crystal stone or bead with them after ritual. They can be sewn up into a small pouch or put on a piece of jewelry. For example, you can braid or thread a bead into a bracelet or anklet. For a seed or stone, you can get some wire and bend it into a small cage for the item, suspending that cage from a chain. The idea is to keep the "seed" close to you for the time you have pledged.

Time and energy should be put into bringing into creation what you have sworn to the Goddess. It can be a work of art or a service performed for the community. It may be an aspect of your own life that you wish to focus on more, such as being more forgiving or at peace, more forceful or daring. You could also take a class or two, finish a project you've been putting off, or learn a new skill or language.

Art can take many forms, but in this case there should be a goal, such as creating gifts for your friends or family for Yule or May Day, making enough pieces to put on a gallery show, or learning

74

a new artistic form or technique. Some examples of services for the community include creating a new study or discussion group, leading a large open ritual, planning an event, starting up a local newsletter, or doing all sorts of charity work. You can also plan on spending more time with an elderly relative, with your children, nieces, nephews and so on, or by becoming a mentor to others.

Changing your life is rather more difficult than taking a class, but you can start small by making peace with someone you've been at odds with, doing something you've been afraid to do, or deliberately altering how you would normally react to an event in your life. Everything begins with a seed that can be tended to so that they will grow into something new, something that will benefit both your life and the lives of those around you.

Flowers of Blood Ritual

For this ritual, have four Quarter candles ready to be lit, plus a statue of Aphrodite on the altar. If you don't have a statue, a large shell will do. Have a candle before the statue or shell, as well.

Place a large bowl filled with water to the West, near the West candle if possible. A clear glass bowl is best. If you want, you can drape the golden net over the bowl for the time being. Have long ribbons of red, pink, gold and purple wrapped around the base of the bowl, enough for at least two ribbons for each person.

You will also need red and purple flowers for this rite, roses and violets if possible. Real flowers are best, but you can use plastic ones if need be. Roses and violets and hyacinths are flowers which were created by the blood of sacrifice.

Cast a circle as usual.

The Priest or a chosen person goes around and lights the North candle, saying:

Silence

He lights the East candle saying:

Song

He lights the South candle saying:

Strength

He lights the West candle saying:

Sorrow

He lights the central candle, the one next to the statue of the Goddess and then stands, holding the taper up over the altar, saying:

From the dark he comes
Your beloved
From the earth he springs
Green and gold
We are as he
And we beloved of thee
Aphrodite
Shall also rise
Yours is the love beyond death
And as we know that love
We shall never die

Hand out a red or purple flower to each person. Before the flower is given to the person, they should be asked:

What is beauty?

All should respond with what immediately springs to mind, what feels right to them. It could be a place, a color, a person, an idea, a time, an Art. There are no wrong answers. Each person should concentrate on putting this into the flower they hold, especially the emotional intensity it brings.

When all are done, the last of the flowers should be placed before the statue of Aphrodite or by the shell that represents Her.

The Priest and Priestess or two people chosen for the task bring around saltwater and incense, blessing each person as is said:

What is beauty
But She
Who are we
But beauty
Proud and graceful
We shall bow to no one
Save those with the virtues
Of the heavens
We shall honor our own
The living and the dead
So that the blood may bloom again
And always
Dumuzi
Adoni
Tzahranos
Osiris
We will walk in your footsteps
Upon the shores of the Goddess
Salt and smoke
Our hearts a rose

Each person kisses the flower they hold and takes turns placing it in the large bowl of water set to the West and taking two ribbons from those wrapped around its base. They say:

To the waters
And from the waters
Is the world renewed
We will remember always

All return to hold hands around the circle, saying:

Dumuzi
Adoni
Tzahranos
Osiris

Yours is the love of beauty
Enough to die for
Let we be
Half as daring

Dance around the circle, a whirling dance if possible, the ribbons swirling around your bodies and between you as you move. The dance should go around at least seven or nine times, but it can go until the energy peaks, when all should sink to the ground and send energy at the statue or shell of Aphrodite, feeding the Goddess.

Feasting in circle is a good idea after this, especially food that reminds you of sacrifices made.

Invocation of Aphrodite

This can be used to call Aphrodite into a circle to witness or to bless the rite with Her attentions. It can also be used to invoke the Goddess into a Priestess so that She can speak directly to those in the circle. If you wish to use a wand for the invocation, it may be decorated with shells or pearls. The best wand would be made from a piece of driftwood.

To set the mood, the incense to be used should be floral but not cloyingly so. A good choice would be a Venus incense. Venus oil can also be used to dress the wand beforehand, charging it with the signature energy of the Goddess.

If the invocation is to be used to invoke the Goddess into a Priestess, have her stand with her hands crossed over her chest, her head bowed, while the invoking person says:

> **Queen of the sea**
> **Perfect and true**
> **By the wave washing on the shore**
> **Wearing it away**
> **By the current in the depths**
> **The rush and the tide**
> **Of power and your need**
> **As it rises within**
> **As it stirs without**
> **A whirlpool**
> **A tempest**
> **A storm**
> **Come to us**
> **Aphrodite**
> **Show us what is right**
> **Teach us of what is most beautiful**
> **We cry to you**

Upon the shell of self
And the pearl that lies
Within the pain
The dark taste
And the name of boundless ecstasy
We bid you near
We whisper your name

All whisper Her name over and again until She is there.

A large shell can be also set at the feet of the Priestess at this point or the person invoking can put a smaller one into the hands of the Goddess. Additionally, a veil can be placed over the head of the Priestess or a longer piece of mostly transparent blue or silver or pale gold cloth can be draped over her entire body. You can use a pearl and shell crown or the golden net tied around her hips.

Symbols of Aphrodite

Aphrodite's symbol is the scalloped shell. Other symbols for Her include a golden net, the image of sea spray, pearls, sparrows, grey doves or grey dove feathers. Flower petals and salt can be placed in a large shell with a pink or white or gold candle. Necklaces of pearls or shells or any piece of jewelry made with pearls or shells make good choices.

You can use a statue of Aphrodite or Venus or even a picture of Her. Postcards or pictures a beautiful ocean view can be used, or any other nature picture that you find inspiring, even if it's not of the sea.

"Where I walk, you may walk. Where I go, you may go. The air of the world is perfumed and the taste of it something you may never forget, no matter how long you linger on the shores of the dead. We who come from below the waves, we remember death better than you for we have not swallowed forgetfulness. We have chosen to drink not from that cup.

You, you who drank and who returned across the river, it is we who remain who must admire such bravery. The world is sharp and the blood precious. You are all precious to us and though we serve, we but serve in different ways. Your way is not our way, but all ways are needed to serve the whole.

Look in one direction and you can see far. Look in all directions and you can see farther, but few may walk but one path at a time. This comes later. That is part of what you strive to attain, and in the attaining gain the greater power of choice, the same choice as those you name the Gods enjoy.

I am not the sea. I am not the waves. I am not love. I am the blood of the sea, the crush of the waves, the desperation of love. I am the blackness which eats the reluctant heart. I am death's lover, but then who is not?"

Aphrodite

Part Two
Cerridwen

Potions

Black steel
And iron cauldron
The core of a fallen star
Fashioned to glory and to the fear of man
Three drops
Form the tender taste of ecstasy
Transformation the terror and the joy combined
Pain creates
What has never been before
What should have been
The truth remains.

No more to hide in the dark
Light gleams from the heart of the cavern
Where she stands with a spoon of horn
In one hand
And a sharp blade in the other
Lit by pearl pale liquid
Moving with a life all its own
Casting shadow across the walls
Creatures stir and emerge from the depths
Rough and damp
Wet from birth
They see their secret mother
Rubbing up against her
Seeking her hand on their nape
She who loves and she who destroys
One and the same.

Black hair streaked white
An iron crown frames a ruby moon
A belt of shell borrowed from the sea
Never to be returned

Beautiful and sorrowful
One moment old
And one moment young
She breathes in the message of the salt winds
Walks upon the midnight shores
Picking up driftwood and polished glass
Green and blue and pale
The fallen feather of a bird
The wandering dreams of men
All to go in the cauldron
Never to return again
Never to be lost.

Heat rises
Serpent one moment and eagle the next
Water falls to steep within the cave
Gleaming on the rocks below
Fire flares up
Green fire then blue
White within and black without
Just as a stone may be split apart
To reveal the greatest of all secrets within
The true and golden heart.

In the darkness, in the tidal caverns near the haunted shores of time, She crouches down in the damp and traces out riddles in the mud. Her hair is long, braided with all manner of found and stolen and lost and forgotten objects—broken shells, misplaced buttons, beads and feathers, fragments of bone. She has waited in the cave a long time and it is there that men seek her out, demanding that She give to them what they most desire.

She laughs at that. Men can be such fools, though She loves them still.

As She draws her spells in the wet earth, fire flares up behind her. The wood burns damply here, green and blue more than red and gold, though its heart remains the same blinding white flame. A great shape sits above it, massive and heavy, far too heavy for any mortal to ever lift and made by no mortal hands. Ancient and black, pitted with countless centuries of use, you might call it a cauldron, but perhaps it is better termed a *caldera*, the place where furious forces rise and swirl together, creating something one moment and tearing it apart the next.

The fire and the sea are contained within it, primal powers in conflict that help mold and shape the Earth. But the cauldron also has its origin among the stars and the breathless cold depths of space resound within it. Light shimmers faintly across the black surface, only to be swallowed up again. But what shines inside it cannot be quelled, cannot be denied—bright, molten, solid, liquid, it seems the very blood of the heavens.

Despite the flames below, the surface of the cauldron is cold, desperately icy to the touch. Bare skin would freeze to it in an instant, yet She strokes it possessively, tracing out the emblems on its surface. They are old, almost worn away, strange, fixed and yet seeming to be constantly in flux. Some might call them runes and others signs, constellations and sigils, but above all they are the visible measure of a spell.

They are a charm, an incantation, names and not-names, all at the same time. They gleam with the rising heat, each one a story, a myth, a legend, a dream passing into existence and then abruptly blown out again, although never to be entirely forgotten. Men have dreamed these dreams. They have spoken and sung of them, and yet none has seen where they lead, what they mean, and from whence they came, for to either side they stretch into the greater dark, the infinite Void, the devourer.

Small figures gather at the edge of the cave, tiny child-size figures. They're scattered in the darkness, as intimate a part of the night as any shadow. They huddle near each other and move in waves, never alone, never apart. They await a word, a command, a spell, a clear demand. Their voices are soft, a whispering echo, the sound of geese flying at night or hounds baying on the hunt through the oldest forest. They have been known by many names, but their own language is beyond human ability voice, just as their hearts appear alien.

"My demons, my hounds, my charge," She says to them and they flow out and around her, a ripple, the beginnings of a wave, a storm. "Go and teach men of their fears, of what the shadows hide. Show them that they are not alone masters of their own fate, nor that dreams cannot still bite and sting."

The little ones swirl and spin faster and faster around Her, a maelstrom, a sucking current, the darkness begging to drag you down to the monster waiting below, to the open mouth. They buzz and they howl as they flow out of the cave, their black eyes burning as cold as the cauldron of their Mistress. They sing with the Abyss, smelling of damp and of death, sweet and earthy and sour.

They are glad to go. They are glad to have something to do. It's what they're made for, because they've always been the builders and the chasers. As they go, flowing along the lines of current from the sea to the land, they transform and become hounds, great black dogs and thin white whippets with red-dipped ears; the hounds of Faery, the haunters in the dark. They howl and She smiles as she dips a carved spoon into the heart of the cauldron, stirring and stirring - a maelstrom, a torrent, a whirlpool, a hurricane.

Outside, the tides begin to roll, the sea on the move, while the moon changes from white to black and finally to beast-red. Hunter's moon, the color of sacrifice. The feast is about to begin.

Transformation is at hand. The spoon stirs the light and the light spills out, but who will dare to drink of what it contains.

Who will dare to play?

Cold Iron and Creation

Cracked and caustic
The fire runs
Runic incantations
The voice of the Gods
Thunder and despair united
The charge of lightning flare to joy
Jagged and direct
It wakes or it destroys
Horn and bone
The great spear crackles
Striking deep
Remaining still
As all around it spins
One face then another passing away
Feathered fanged
Naked furred and scaled
She the Lady of transformation
Long braided hair
Double tailed
By the moon bemused
No simple dream
Beware beware

The broken bones of the sea cave stand sentinel, weed and sea brack forming a curtain over cracked stone. Sometimes, the entrance is damp, the tides having withdrawn to the deeper part of the ocean, and sometimes it's completely engulfed in the cool green-grey waters. Storm tide waters, flush with white foam and restless, they are both beautiful and merciless, tasting of the unknown depths from which they were born.

Their mistress knows their humors well, for She shares in them. Just as She is acquainted with the dank, cool heart of the cave, the darkness that protects the treasures of the sea. They are a part of Her, even as She stares into the great black cauldron, seeing everything and seeing nothing in what it contains. The cauldron is huge, ancient beyond measure, pitted by the passage of countless centuries. It's all of one piece, made of a metal from beyond the Earth, a fallen piece of the sky, iron and yet not iron.

It's this iron that is meant when people claim that those of Faery fear cold steel, black iron. Not the iron that humans forge into tools and weapons, but the iron that symbolizes the weight of the human condition and the physical plane. The iron that binds what was once free to the chains of the Earth, keeping spirit anchored within the body. It's a willing enough decision, of course, but not an easy one. Sometimes it's just painful to take on form and substance, to feel so very much, even if it was a choice you wanted.

Iron keeps and it holds. It provides necessary weight. Not surprisingly, there is the common phrase that says some people have an *iron will*. Will is the iron that keeps us in our bodies, the same will which allowed us to be born back this world in the first place. Small wonder then, that iron and steel form one of the tools of the modern Witch, a focus passing through the blade representing their purpose and intent. In the distant past, the blades were made of stone, black stone, but the idea remains the same.

The cauldron of Cerridwen is made of iron and not, of earth and not. It's metal and stone, and not. As it fell to the Earth it flamed white-hot, and when it cooled at the last, it turned black, though what it contains remained white. White and lustral and liquid and pure, it's a drink meant to intoxicate, a drink that awakens the senses. It can even make the spirit drunk.

This, then, is the cauldron of the Muse, the cauldron of Cerridwen. It's the cauldron of wisdom and of inspiration, of birth and re-birth. It holds the white-hot core of a star, a living essence, the spark of possibility. Like the cauldron, all living things contain a spark, a brilliant ember of light borrowed from the Source. We all live and die, sinking down within the cauldron, only to be stirred back up from the depths once more.

The legend of Cerridwen tells us that She was mother to two children, a daughter and a son, one extraordinarily beautiful and one supremely ugly. She wanted to conjure a special drink for the ugly child to make up for his lot in life and so brewed one up in Her cauldron. But, it had to be stirred for a year and a day before it would be any good. She employed Gwion, a local boy, to stir the contents, never wavering, unrelentingly, until at the last three magickal drops were created. He either drank them then or had them accidentally fall on him. But, of course, there are no real accidents. Either way, once he tasted of the cauldron, he could see all things, including the fact that Cerridwen would not be pleased at what had just transpired.

Gwion knew what would happen in the end, but still he ran because he feared losing his old life. Cerridwen chased him and Gwion made use of his new understanding to change shape again and again in a vain effort to elude Her, transforming from hare to fish to bird, Earth, Water, Air. But, of course, Cerridwen knew that trick and transformed Herself from greyhound to otter to hawk. In the end, as was meant to be, She caught him and ate him, as Gwion took the form of a seed—a seed which was the spark of Fire—and She that of a black hen.

The Goddess says: *"my story lies only half-told, a remnant of what was. The boy who tended the cauldron was father to the man, as I am mother to the daughter who weds the king and knows the land. So I step, so I travel from fire to water to earth, making passage from blood to living clay."*

This seed took hold inside Her and Cerridwen became the mother of Gwion's second life, not just as an ordinary man this time, but one with the ability to create with words—otherwise known as incantations or spells—and who had the gift of knowing called the Sight or the Second Sight. For to drink from the cauldron, to undergo the process of transformation, and to be born again is to become a Shining One. This was how Gwion became one of the greatest bards of all time, Taliesin.

She was both the death and the life of him, the means by which he was torn apart and rebuilt, a shamanic transformation that freed his voice and power, that turned a boy into a man and a man into a magician. Cerridwen served the purpose of the cauldron as much as the mysterious potion. Because it's of little use to taste the drink of the Gods, without having undergone the struggle which lends itself to understanding. We must not only be able to drink, but be ready to drink.

As Cerridwen Herself puts it *"I wear no mask, for all my faces are masks and I am they. I change and change not, as you must. Thus the moon has long been a mask for many you name as Goddess, for though the moon alters, it yet remains. My symbol lies not in the moon, but closer to its shadow. For shadows also alter with the light and so find their opposite in the light, they with whom are a match.*

They say I have borne two children, a boy and a girl child, one precious and lovely and the other horrid and undesirable. They, too, are shadows—shadows of what others would see in me and, even more, in their own selves. They two must become as one, shadow and light, male and female, what is thought of as fair and what is considered to be foul—only then will the way be made clear and the door open."

Cerridwen most likely takes Her name from the Welsh *cerdd* and *wen*, meaning "gain" and "white." The word *cerdd* also has an association with the Arts and the Craft, particularly the idea of being clever or crafty. The whiteness that is gained is not just perfection, but the white blood of the Otherworld, of the Queen of Faery, and, of course, the moon. The *cutty sark* is also said to be white, the terrible sow who is emblem of death, what no one will escape at the last. She is the eater of life and the giver of life. Not always a pleasant path, but a necessary experience, especially if you want to be born to knowledge, to learn how to stand with one foot in this world and one foot in another.

Her fabulous cauldron resides at *Caer Sidi* or *Caer Sidhe*, the spinning castle for the spinning Fey, the little ones who build and who whirl. *Caer Sidhe* is also a name for the Otherworld, the Underworld, the realm of the dead. Other names for this place include the Castle or House of Arianrhod, the *Corona Borealis*, or the Crown of the North Wind. It's also known as the Crown of Crete or Ariadne's Crown, Ariadne being one of Cerridwen's sister-selves. This starry crown was fashioned from the wedding crown of Dionysus and Ariadne, seven gems to create seven stars, just as one of the oldest labyrinths has seven rings.

As Cerridwen stirs this cauldron, images rise to the surface only to sink down once more into the depths. Some things take a long time to rise and some never completely surface, often because we simply aren't built to see the whole of them. Some wait a long time for the right moment to be made manifest, while others come much more easily, emerging like the fizzing of bubbles. These are small things mostly, elements that commonly enter our world. Greater things take more time and effort to come into being, countless centuries and even Ages might pass before they take shape. It requires great magick to make great magick and some of these need to be worked by many generations of Witches, each stirring their own cauldron and spinning their own web.

The white glow of what lies within the cauldron is like no other light. It's warm and cool at the same time, a liquid that shimmers and glimmers, moving almost like mercury, the traditional metal of the transformation. It will take the mystical and traditional year and a day before it's ready, only then to yield up it's precious drops of wisdom and inspiration. Three drops, and three drops alone. It may not sound like much, but three is also a mystical number for three makes a binding, connecting one thing to another. One drop for the past, one drop for the future and the third for the eternal now. One for life, one for death and one for rebirth. One for who you are, one for who you were and one for who you will always be, from which both the past and the future are fixed.

Of old, the cauldron also has three attributes. One is how it continually renews itself, that what it contains can never be exhausted. This resembles the cornucopia, the horn of plenty of the she-goat, Almalthea, who nursed the Greek God, Zeus. What the cauldron and the cornucopia give to us is no less than all we require. The horn and the cauldron will never be empty, because they are tied to infinite creation, the web that touches everything and everyone. They represent channels through which power freely pours through all of time and space, Seen and Unseen.

The cauldron also has powers over life and death, over regeneration. Some stories relate how it can bring the dead back to life, most especially great warriors and heroes. A form of the transformative ability was given to Gwion after he "accidentally" tasted the contents of the cauldron. To alter from one state to another, one form to another, one world and one life to another, shows that there are many aspects to us and to reality itself. There are levels, layers, aspects, attributes, incarnations, all swirling and whirling around us, while only thing remains constant—the core of who and what we are. We are surrounded by spirits and movement, yet the eye of the storm lies within us, waiting to be tapped.

This still eye, this core, our star, the ember of our self, passes through the cauldron again and again, cloaking itself in different times, forms, names, and places. We spring from the same seed, each time learning new lessons, being given new opportunities to explore, as well as to provide the world what we are meant to provide. We are continuously following in the footsteps of Gwion, seeking to discover within us our own bright Taliesin. We both need to spin and to be still, a key to the old magicks.

Lastly, the cauldron provides inspiration. Inspiration is also creative power, a force that can bring new worlds into being and alter old ones. Equally inexhaustible and transformational in nature, inspiration is perhaps the greatest aspect of the cauldron, as it is the greatest aspect of the Muse. To taste of the cauldron is to taste of the fire of inspiration and be branded by it, unable to return to what we once were. More than that, unwilling to go back to anything less. It's to find the desire within us to express that fire, no matter the cost, no matter the sacrifice. What else can matter when you are blinded and burnt by bliss and would do almost anything to remain?

A fourth aspect to the cauldron might be conceived of, though, rounding out the powers to four instead of the traditional three, and that is the attribute of magick. Certainly, cauldrons tend to be where Witches cook up their potions and spells, a focus for curses, cures, and stirring desires into being. It can contain intent until it's time to be released, wreaking havoc or bounty, storms of necessary destruction for the new life to come. The cooking pot of the Witch is the cauldron in all its phases, a place to stir new realities into being.

Magick, inspiration, transformation, renewal...the cauldron is a microcosm of the universe. It's both the womb and the tomb out of which we may be born to either this world or to the realm of Faery, of death. It's the chalice of the volcano, the bowl of the world's oceans from which life first sprang. It's the mother of all waters, the currents which run through all times and all worlds, weaving the all into one and the one into all. It's also the body of the cunning ones, keeping their bright blood with its own inherent vitality of creation and destruction, cousin to the white fluid shared by the Fey and by the stars.

In Scandinavian mythology, the cauldron is the source of all the world's rivers. These rivers, depending on whether they are "male" or "female," form boundaries and wellsprings. They map out the land, the lines unseen save for those who have gained the ability to see as the Fey see. This rushing water, this surging energy, helps to create the literal and metaphysical world we all live in; they are the roaring veins of the Earth. For without water, as without the energy that infuses the blood and brings it to life, nothing living would remain.

As the God of the West is the lord of death and the world beyond this one, so the Goddess of the West, the Muse, is the river of the creative spirit, the passion of the heart, and the consummation of the Arts. Cerridwen's cauldron is one such projection of this passion, a deep and eternally renewing source of fertility, power, and inspiration. When linked to the South-West, to the fire and water found within the blood, transformation is not just possible, but inevitable. Though, like a blade, it is double-edged, cutting within and without; eminently capable of harming or healing or doing both as is sometimes needed.

Cerridwen tells us *"They say the cauldron is mine, but that is not strictly so—for I **am** the cauldron. I am made to hold the flame, the drink of life and light and powerful things, of the dying and dreams of mankind. To taste of my drink **is** to die. It is to be born. It is to fall and to rise, as all must fall and rise that is living. It is to know pain so great that you wish to die and cannot. It is to know joy so strong that you wish to live forever and cannot. It is the moment caught between the two.*

Drink, drink—for where shall you find a better cup than this? For the cup and the cauldron are as one, though one is of the Gods and one a gift to man. But then why not die? Why not live? Why not drink and drink deep…drink until naught remains, until all.

I am black iron and I am steel. I am the dark where you fear to tread, though tread you must and will, for such were you made—to drink and to dare what even the Gods would not."

Gwion was reborn because he drank of the cauldron. He was reborn as Taliesin. It's said he gained the power of the Muse from Cerridwen's cauldron, but it might better be said that he was eaten up and reborn from the Muse, making him capable of being a channel for Her Arts. He let the power of the cauldron begin to flow through him, bringing with it gifts of knowledge, beauty, charm, and passion. Not painlessly, of course, for he paid a steep price for this new life, not the least having to die to do it. In the story, it was a literal death, but that doesn't mean we don't face death in seeking to taste of the cauldron—occasionally, an actual life-and-death experience might result but, more commonly, a death involving all we have known and done and felt before, which can be just as painful.

This illustrates that if we wish to transform the world, we first need to transform ourselves. Because, when we dare to channel untamed forces into reality, stuffing them into forms way too small for them, the effort changes not just reality but the one did the work. The very act of channeling, of allowing these energies to flow through us, can't help but change us. The greater the force that we attempt to bring to life, the greater the risk it will entail, but also the greater the transformation it will etch within our bodies, minds, and hearts. It will also end up having a wider impact on the world we live in.

We have to learn to bear the pain. We have to be capable of not only looking within the workings of the universe, but within ourselves. We can't have one without the other. To be a Witch, to be cunning, we have to *ken*, meaning understanding by simply understanding, sensing what is really real. We can't have that without aiming it at what makes us tick. How can we look behind the illusion if we allow illusions to rule our lives. We must be ruthless as well as compassionate, a heady combination.

101

Cerridwen talks about this price: *"My symbol is not the moon, but what eats the moon. The living shadow, the dream of death. I am no less beautiful than my sister-self, yet men fear me, as they fear the dark and less merciful side not only of the great divine but of their own natures, be they divine or not. But I say that beauty is not mercy nor is it merciful, for in shadow may sleep be found and peace, and the light can burn as much as illuminate. Still, do not fear to grasp the light, though do not forget that to grasp the light is to take hold of the dark, that both have gifts for thee, that both require sacrifice."*

Cerridwen may have white in Her name, but black becomes Her, as well. She is Queen of the Chessboard of night and day, of light and dark, of life and death, where a move on one side mirrors the other. She is the Lady of the Castle at the edge of the sea, a castle that's also black and white, a castle from which howls the winds of the dead, sometimes giving and sometimes hungry. She stands at the edge of the unknown without, the seeking after, the journey within. The first of many journeys, each built upon the last and increasingly challenging.

This is the price of the cauldron. To dare to drink something that you cannot *un*drink, that you cannot go back from. To decide not just to be changed, but to become an agent of change, a *heretic* in the old meaning of the word—one who chooses. What we choose is the brightest star in the sky, the farthest horizon. To wish upon a star is not just some wistful, childish fancy but a metaphor for picking the brightest thing in all the world, or in all the worlds, that we will never let go, that we will follow no matter where it takes us.

Cerridwen says: *"you who see me as a crone know me not, for I am not some wizened hag ready but to be cast into the fire. Men made me to be so, for they feared my beauty, my excesses, my visions. When I come to you I come in the night. I whisper at first, but beware that my whisper does not come to a shout."*

Once we have drunk, once we have sworn, once we have taken that first step, it's time to really start paying attention. After all, there's no turning back. The coming transformation comes on like a runaway train, a tornado, an angry Goddess. The warning being that She just may hunt down those unwise to drink without first purifying themselves to the task. Whether they actually knew what they were signing on for is no excuse. Gwion probably had no clue what would happen when he tasted those infamous three drops, and then it was too late. There was no escape. He ran straight to his death, straight to the bleak embrace of the tomb, and was reborn from the equally dark womb, becoming a great man of vision, yes, but no longer who he had been. Are we prepared to give up as much, not knowing the outcome?

Not only can we undergo the test of the cauldron, though, we can become as the cauldron. Cerridwen had two children, twins, one beautiful and one ugly. These two children represent the twinned aspects of beauty and of terror, of ecstasy and fear, ancient gateways to this world and the realm of Faery. Like the cauldron, we can also be the understanding of that connection, a gateway between the two, the mouth of the hollow hill, the dark well and bogs where the ancients offered blood and gold and bone.

We can be a force of life and breath, of death and dream, letting the currents that flow between the Seen and Unseen flow through us. We can become a bridge, one of the gifts that the Muse offers us. Not an easy or comfortable gift to accept, but well worth the risk, the pain and the struggle, for it leads not just to the Sight, but to an experience of this life at its best. We can be charmed by it as we can charm others, not only have attained the secrets, but becoming one with them.

Cerridwen asks: *"What would you have me tell you? All the secrets of the universe? The secrets of all time? Even if I knew them, I would not tell you. For in the telling they grow cold and can no longer warm what needs to be warmed. Ask my sister if you do not believe me, She*

103

who keeps the oldest and the coldest secrets of all. Just as She keeps those which yet burn, which would burn you to ash and dust if you but set a single drop to your tongue. Those secrets are like my own, secrets that must burn. Secrets that you must feel to know. Secrets you would die to attain, and some that you must die to attain."

Only then can we become lit from within, capable of speaking with the voice of divine authority. We can be the singer and the song, the dancer and the dance, a radiant poet capable of great acts of magick. We become our own beginning and our own ending, living in the world in full knowledge of that circle. Our words can become imbued with the power of understanding, spells to make and unmake. We don't just speak the truth anymore, we speak prophecy, the truth of the Gods. The spell of the Witch no longer just a hope, no longer even focused intent, but the absolute will of Fate. We become as Fate, because we know what Fate is and our place in the pattern it weaves. The one true thing.

As Cerridwen tells us *"we transform, but that which remains true to us…remains. The boy alters, shifting from one form to the next, before at the last becoming a seed. A seed such as a God would provide. This seed is what grew into a man within the cauldron, a second birth to the world of light and understanding.*

To speak with the voice of the God, the voice of wind and waters and of the deepest channels of the earth, that is what may be gained in coming to the light and allowing it to become as your self. We all have a seed. We all have a minute particle of light, the same light which feeds the visible stars, the same power and force that the heavens provide.

But many fear the little death. They fear the chase, the black, the depths, the cauldron. They fear me, for I become as that fear and I chase and chase and chase and none may escape me. Not those who run, nor those who cower, and not even those who stand and face me unafraid. For this is my gift, and none may remain in this place and not change, not unless it is true death they seek."

Inspiration and awareness, the sort of extrasensory awareness that is equated to the Sight, are intimately interconnected. To be inspired is to be awake and aware of what is really going on all around us, especially what we're normally unaware of. When we awaken by passing through the cauldron, we find ourselves able to glimpse the real beauty of existence. The Veil parts, both the one that obscures the vision of our own experience and the Veil which separates this place from the Otherworld. We and the dead, we and those of Faery who are our kin, are not so very different. One crucial difference between us lies in the ability to see.

The veil is mainly forgetfulness. It's the illusion of separation. For all that separates the living from the dead is the dream of time, the belief that we cannot see or sense each other. Those on the other side, those who are *dead*...they are not truly dead but have passed to another form of life. True death is, rather, not being; to have your particular thread ripped out of the tapestry of the all. It is to never have been, not just being unable to be reborn, but not having been ever born before.

We're all part of a great tapestry, of the web of stars, our knot of light shining in conjunction with countless others, connected to them across time and space. This web contains worlds within worlds, Seen and Unseen, physical and metaphysical. Sometimes, our thread lies close to others for a time, only to drift away from them. Sometimes, we are braided together forever, traveling from life to life with those we have known before. We are kin, companions, mother and father to each other, brother, sister, son, daughter, husband, wife. Clan, family, coven, our blood is bound together along with the land that we have shared it with.

What can we see in the cauldron if not all we have been. Our life now, our past, our future, it doesn't matter once we can see into that mirror, into that pool, the well of self. We seek to know our spirit, not just the one we have now, but the greater spirit that we are always a part of. This spirit has a consciousness of its own and we help make that consciousness as we are made by it. We are many and one and, in this way, reflect the universal web, the Wyrd.

Cerridwen tells us *"there are many cauldrons, some large and some small, but all reflect the greater one—the cauldron of the sky and the cauldron of the cup of the earth. This is not my cauldron to tend, though all cauldrons but remain the same cauldron, large or small, the circle which contains. One life passing to another, also completing a circle. While the greater wisdom lies within, the centermost point, the kernel of truth, the seed of life and love and self, the northern star."*

The outside of the cauldron is not necessarily pretty because it's the inside that matters and cradles the gift that will forever alter our lives. To drink from the cauldron is to be shattered, to be torn apart, to be devoured and spat out again, all the stronger. We dare our death and dismemberment and find ourselves pieced back together again, only somewhat…different this time. Part of that difference lies in the fact that we have faced death, gone through it, and emerged on the other side. We chose to embrace the cycle and take a conscious role in it, yet we also emerge different because some small part of us never really succeeds in leaving the realm of death.

This new-old self still has one foot forever in the Otherworld, a link that can lead us there and back again. We can use this for communicating with spirits and entities, even the Gods, and for spells, healing magick, divination, and for guidance and divination. We have seen the fire, eaten of the fire, and had it not just consume us but give rise to our resurrection. This is the fire that burns in the hearts of all who have undergone the journey of transformation. It's the gold of the sun that normally sleeps beneath the mountains, below the hills. The secret treasure, the fallen seed of the stars, what Prometheus, what Lucian, the Light-Bringer gained at great price.

It is Witchfire, this living flame. Not that everyone doesn't have a flame inside them, a fire connected to the Source. But the living flame has become conscious of us as we have become conscious of it. The fire within the blood, the crown upon the heart, and in many ways, the true seat of consciousness. In Eastern symbolism, the heart chakra lies at the midpoint between the lower (physical) chakras and the upper (ethereal) chakras. It's through the heart that the worlds above and the worlds below meet and find their balance. The heart forms the bridge and that bridge is love, the blossoming fire.

It is up to us. It's up to us to dare to drink, to dare to decide, to dare to transform our world and to be transformed. What world do we want to live in? The first step towards that world lies in how we think and feel and perceive and believe in the world. No lasting change can happen without a corresponding inner transformation. To be born a second time while still alive, to have a new world rise up from the ashes of the old, the old must first be destroyed. The fire must burn away all that is not required, so that we can be reborn.

The old secrets of the art of alchemy really didn't have much to do with the outer world, transmuting lead into gold, but were about a more important inner transmutation. We start out like lead, heavy and stolid, based in the Earth and Water which is flesh, only to seek after the spiritual flames where Air and Fire meet and mingle and become one. But that is only the beginning of a long, strange trip. We build our foundation so that the tower can come next, so we can travel not just up our internal rainbow but to find the rainbow bridge of the Gods. The rainbow that is a pole and a tree and a promise, entwined by twin snakes.

Fire and Ice

The very bones and skull and blood
The itching madness
Of each and every poet
Scribbling away
Their pens the press of waves
Their words the storm
The arching fire
Splitting the sky and the sea
They will know
And yearn to serve you
As no other

What does the cauldron contain? Everything and nothing. What do you see when you look into it? Everything and nothing. You choose what you take away from the experience of the cauldron. You choose and are chosen, for once you have *seen* the cauldron is now of you and those who come after may drink of you and know the cauldron through that. This is the spell of the cauldron pouring forth from one to another, never-ending, never-ceasing, water which is not water, light which is not light, flame which is not flame, creation which continues to create.

We all seek to become the Phoenix, rising up from lead and ash to become what we were always meant to be, a shining star, as dread and mysterious as any of the Gods above or below. This is potential, hope, the gift of choice, and the yearning for more which is an inherent part of human nature. However, it's Witches, Shamans, magicians, and mystics everywhere who must lead the way, vanguards of truth, guardians of the great journey, and instigators of evolution.

We seek the fire, the light, the power which rains down from the heavens and marks us as its own. One symbol of old for this power was the Phoenix and another was the dragon, for as Cerridwen tells us "*a dragon is a serpent of water and of flame, a creature of the blood and of the gold hidden in the blood. The gold which is the sun's gift to the earth, not a gold of metal but of light of which the metal is only a physical reminder.*

The gold of kings and of the wisdom of kings, the wisdom of the sun in the earth, the fire in the flesh. My art is a dragon-sign, the blaze which is the mark of blood. I am water, but not water. Blood, but not blood alone. The blood that is also flame, just as the cauldron holds water that is not water."

This Phoenix fire can be found within the authority of the word, the mystery of the spell, song and sounds tied to intent and emotion. Incantation is one of the old gifts granted by the Muse and with that ability we can channel the words as much as recite them, using them as a focus for the might to make something real or to change what is. We channel the magick which gives the word its spark, its meaning, knowing what connects the word to the thing itself.

This is one reason why the true names of the Gods are often kept secret, for once the name of a thing is known the one who knows it can claim power and dominium over it. We can conjure up a spirit and control it so long as we knew its true name and, accordingly, its essence. Witches of old used to keep their true names hidden for the same reason. They only shared their true name—and thus their power—with those they trusted with their lives and more, with their very spirit. Covens also kept secret their real names. The outward name simply shows the outward mask, usually just the locale that the coven was in charge of and the land it was bound to.

In order to create something we have to give it a name and so form. In order to alter something we have to know its true name and gain power over it. We need to utterly understand its essence to be able to shift the shape that it has taken in this world, to alter the projection. Ideas take on many forms, reflecting not just the times but the culture, the necessities of the moment.

For example, the living concept of the spirit of Freedom has taken on many forms and will take on many more in the future. It's been associated with different Gods and Goddesses and legendary heroes, whether mythological or symbolic, from Lady Liberty (pre-curser to the Statue of Liberty) to Marianne, the heroine who represented the French Revolution. But then Freedom in the Piscean Age tended to focus on the concept of this versus that—conservative and liberal, peasants and nobles, haves and have-nots—the metaphor of conflict.

What Freedom will look like in the Aquarian Age is something entirely new. Rather than the Piscean push-pull, up-down, right-wrong, Aquarius means a rather more holistic view, toleration and acceptance and trying to see how all the puzzle pieces fit together. What names, what heroes, what Gods and Goddesses and legends this Freedom will gather as it coalesces remains to be seen. But one thing is true and that is we will all play our part in contributing to its new form, in giving it a name.

What is a name? What is the word that creates? The name and the word is the point of the power that extends from the Source, passing from eternity to the realm of time, from formlessness to form, from that which has no physicality to that which does. When something is named this becomes the final connection. The name it's given shapes, in part, how it will appear here at the last and can, in turn, affect the spiritual realm it originally sprang from.

The Muse offers us the gift of the word. By the use of conjurations, spells, charms, and incantations, we can call up powers and focus them on what we wish to create and to change. We pull something wet and wriggling up out of the cauldron, a formless thing that takes shape as we name it. We give form to the formless, using the Arts we have been taught and the rough magick which flows through those Arts.

Cerridwen's *"dreams are forged of stout things. They do not shiver and break at the slightest wind, at the merest word. My art is made of blood, cast of the flames wherein all is first come to creation, and when they emerge from the forge they are too bright to behold, too beautiful to deny."*

Not that it's ever an easy task to bring something new into being. Part of that travail involves spinning it out of our own desires, our own being. When we give birth to a new form, we are its parents and we bear that responsibility and pain. What happens after that we have less say over for, once here, these forms are conscious in their own right and will follow the path of their destiny. We can only give them the best beginning, the best start that we can.

If we catch hold of the images swirling in the liquid of the cauldron we can give them life. The cauldron is as much a source of gifts as the box of Pandora was, Pandora meaning the all (pan) and gift (dora). Though, like the legend of Pandora, Cerridwen and Her cauldron carry a warning—that not all gifts are to the good and not all gifts will be easily accepted. The one who brings gifts may be welcomed for it or they might be condemned. Not only that, those same gifts they agonized and sweated over might not end up being for them to reap the benefits of, but for all those others.

When we delve deeply within ourselves to find these gifts, some will appear as shadow and some as light. There's no telling which we will need the most, not until we pay the price. All will change us and our lives and the lives of those around us. We may not always like that change, especially at first. Even those close to us and who say they are our friends and will support us no matter what, even they may not like where we are going or what we are becoming. They may have to fall away as we undergo the trial of transformation, possibly because they may fear the trials and changes they are themselves busy avoiding. They might tell you that we're wrong or try to hold us back, keeping us as we are, predictable and "safe."

But we must follow where our path is leading us, so long as it's a true voice we are listening to. We must drink from the cauldron and undergo the changes it will bring, even if it may take us to a dark place for a time. There in the dark we can seek the light, the light that is our essence and the secret seed of our soul. The Goddess eats us and gives birth to us, the Goddess who is the cauldron and the cave, womb and tomb. We lie in the darkness, cocooned by it, and are transformed, a painful process but one that's even more painful if we try to avoid it.

When we are reduced to the one thing, that one thing is who we are. It's our light and our spark and our seed and our name—the gem of the crown—and ready to be planted in fertile ground in order to spring forth and grow into a new form. All else coalesces around that single point, projecting back out into the world. All else passes away but that one thing; pain, pleasure, good luck, bad, all our possessions, none of that matters. Nothing lasts for long or can be counted on to last, save that one thing which can never be taken away. Given away, yes, but not taken away. It's the metaphoric pearl worth all the rest.

Gwion was eaten by Cerridwen, but he was killed only to be reborn. There was no other way to get him to where he needed to go, to see him become what he needed to become. To be a Witch or a cunning one we *must* die and be reborn. We are required to seek the depths of the cauldron, the cave, the earth, the tomb, and take hold of the secret fire hidden there. We must drink from the waters of understanding and be remade. We eat the flames and the flames eat us.

Witches transform and travel to the Sabbat, where we learn of magick and interact with the Gods and countless other spirits and beings. Each transformation is a death, a death of the old and a rebirth to the new. It serves as a reminder that the body that we wear is not really who we are, but just a vessel that our spirits use, a touch point to exist here in this world. The fire in the blood is also a touch point, an intimate link to our brothers and sisters who yet reside among the stars. Fire in the water makes up the blood, golden hidden in scarlet, as the blood of the Fey is silver in white.

What we learn from death we make use of in life, as what we experience in life we find faith in while among the dead. Memory binds the two together, memory and affection. We are all one family, Witches, Fey, and Gods and even Lady Fate must acknowledge the strength forged of that singular union. Alone, we do not have the complete makings of the spell required—the charm of knowing, the power of doing, and the art of daring, all are necessary for the song of making, the source of all essence.

A Prayer to Cerridwen

Mother of the moon's shadow
Of red iron
And the dark flash of fire
Where the earth meets
The fallen stone of the sky
The dragon's eye
Green and true
Singed and black
All-seeing
Blind
The charm of the ages
Born of smoke and blood
And the spell of need
Cerridwen awaken
We call upon you
Upon the cross of steel and bone
Wherein all are tested
To stir the fire within the soul
The flame of water
The crying yearning spark
Of which we all
Are descended
And to which we all as yet aspire
We call for the promise to waken
The gift to spin
As your own would spin
Worlds and dreams
Each passing into the other
Some ghosts and some shadows
Fourfold and one

Rite to Ask a Vision of Cerridwen

This can be done either with a circle or without one. If you are doing this with a group of people, the cauldron or bowl will need to be where everyone can easily see into it.

Fill the cauldron (or a black bowl) that you are using to scry with salt water and set it within the circle of four lit candles. Seat yourself before it. You can also choose to surround the cauldron with fresh green leaves and branches, preferably with dew or rain still on them.

An evocation to be used before scrying:

> **Black water**
> **Cool water**
> **Salt water**
> **Sea**
> **Reveal now reveal**
> **What lies beneath**
> **What lies concealed**
> **What must be**
> **Of what men dream**
> **Of what Gods weave**
> **Black water**
> **Cool water**
> **Salt water**
> **Sea**
> **The cauldron of vision**
> **Be now be**

The last six lines of this evocation can also be used as a round.

Note: When you do cauldron rituals, the cauldron can be filled with both water and fire, such as in this case, or with just fire or just water. Water is to see and fire is to know. Water flows out and when you follow you can see all. You can see the currents that lie below the surface of things. When it is filled by fire, you touch upon the fire of the stars, that which burns down to one singular point. Both speak of the same vision, one born of the blood where fire and water reside.

When the cauldron is filled with just water, you might place four lit candles around it. When the cauldron is filled with just fire, you might put four small bowls of water around it. Saltwater would be the best, seawater being another metaphor for blood. Water and salt together is not necessarily a symbol of earth and water as often used in modern pagan rites, but represents blood. We were once marked in our rituals by blood, not blessed by salt and water.

The fire in the cauldron and the water in the cauldron are both different kinds of gates. Cerridwen asks us to make the choice by asking ourselves: "*Where do you seek to go? What do you seek to know? Your self, the true nature of the flame? Or what lies beyond the familiar circle of light, down deep in the dark, there to see yet another sort of self looking back at you. The self of other, that with which you share everything and nothing.*
True scrying is not just to see, but to be..."

Blessing Rite of Cerridwen

Cast circle as usual. Set the cauldron or black bowl in the center of the circle or clear the altar and set the cauldron on it. The cauldron can be decorated with red and gold and yellow ribbons or with white feathers around the base. If it's winter, you can always use evergreen boughs, preferably with the berries still on them.

Small figurines of animals can also be placed around the cauldron—white sows or black hens in particular, or any assortment of white animal, fish, and bird figurines. Figurines made of bone or horn would be appropriate, even a scattering of white bone beads.

Fill the bowl or cauldron with a clear liquid, either water (preferably spring or rain water) or a small amount of a clear alcohol.

These words can be said by one person or be split up among the group. If you wish, each person may place a white bone figurine or bead around the cauldron as they say their portion:

> **Lady of darkness**
> **Lady of light**
> **By that which is stirred**
> **To transformation**
> **To live to die**
>
> **Once more**
> **To face the secret door**
> **And there to take the road within**
> **What lies between**
> **All we know**
> **Seen, unseen**
>
> **We ask of you**
> **A taste of all**

To drink the drink which speaks
Which calls
Which touches worlds above
And worlds below

The living breath
The cauldron keeps
The draught of death
Which wakes to sleep

A taste
A taste
We beg of thee
To rouse the senses
Set us free

You can then repeat these last five lines quietly as each person approaches, still circling, and dips the tip of their finger in the liquid, touching it to their mouth. Continue until everyone has done this three times. One drop is for the past, one for the future, and one for the eternal now that connects them, two coming together to make one.

Afterwards, the group stands in a circle, holding hands around the cauldron, saying:

We come together
We walk alone
We light the path
For those
Who shall come after us

Can you see them?
Can you see them?
Can you see them?
They can see us

Everyone holds their hands towards the cauldron, palms forward, saying:

> **Mother Cerridwen**
> **Bless us**
> **With water**
> **With fire**
> **With all the good**
> **That fills and flows**
> **From your cauldron**
> **The eternal wellspring**

If you desire to invoke Cerridwen at this point, have a Priestess stand in the West of the circle. Move the cauldron to be at her feet or give her the bowl of liquid after you have invoked the Goddess.

Everyone may come before Cerridwen for Her to bestow blessings as desired and any words She may choose to impart. Afterwards, be sure to thank the Goddess for Her presence in the ritual.

After the Goddess has been dismissed, everyone may sit down to feast together. The remains of what is in the bowl and or cauldron should be given to the waters in some way, either a local stream, lake, or river. If you have no way of doing this, libate it to the earth or to a tree as you might normally do.

During this rite, keep in mind what you wish to discover about yourself, about why you are here, and what gift you are meant to bring into the world. All three are really the same question. The answer lies in the cauldron, as it lies sleeping in the center of the maze and within your own secret heart. We already know it, but sometimes we need to be awakened to that knowing. We seek to be reminded of who we are and why we chose to be born again upon the Earth. To drink of the cauldron is to be awakened.

Cauldron of Inspiration Ritual

This rite is meant to help us choose and explore new avenues of self and experience. There are many aspects of life that we spurn or that we haven't brought fully into our lives, sometimes because we just don't have time, but sometimes because we find them a little frightening or are uncertain of them. It's too easy to fall into complacency about all we can do and we might even begin to avoid any experiences that could further our growth and understanding of who we are. We build our own boxes and then live in them, feeling safe there, but if we let that illusion of safety keep us from occasionally choosing to go outside the box, then we've not built a home, but a prison.

If something is holding us back from expressing ourselves, then it is worth taking a second look and deciding if we need to change it and the circumstances of our lives. But sometimes we may not be sure of what to do, where to look, how to try. We may not know what walls have to come down, what battle to fight, not without first getting a taste of what we might be missing? This rite is a way to explore those options.

For example, if you draw the word "inspire" from the cauldron, you can work to allow this virtue to more fully into your life by setting aside an hour each week to do what you are inspired to do. You might take a pottery or painting class, or you may teach a class yourself or take your children or nieces or nephews to a museum. If you pull out "directness" you can work on being more forward, more forceful in your interactions with others, and consider a little less how they might react. Let yourself say what you've always wanted to say, what you might even think needs saying, but have let your uncertainties or concerns over how others might see you hold you back. Don't go crazy, but why not express yourself.

Along the same lines, choosing "grace" might mean taking a dance class or two. You could also take some martial arts or simply practice being more thoughtful in how you move, in how you speak. "Serenity" could allow you to practice more meditation or decide to take some yoga, though even just going for more long walks in some local quiet place and listening to nature can lend itself to becoming more serene.

Fill the cauldron with stones with words (the virtues) written on them. You can also just use slips of folded paper or even those cheap plastic Easter eggs with slips of paper inside. Go ahead and be creative. Tie the papers onto objects if you like or write the virtues on leaves.

Cast a circle as usual. The cauldron filled with the virtues should be set in the middle.

Everyone begins to move slowly around the cauldron. Eventually, when each person feels the time is right, they should place a single flower that they have brought at the base of the cauldron as an offering. It would be best if they were real flowers, but fake ones can be used in a pinch.

A chant that can be used for this if you are using stones:

> **Black as iron**
> **Cold as steel**
> **Burning sun**
> **The truth reveal**
> **By the cauldron**
> **By the stone**
> **Claim the secrets**
> **Make them known**

If you aren't using stones, but strips of paper, then the chant can be changed to:

Black as iron
Cold as steel
Burning sun
The truth reveal
By the cauldron
Shall it be known
Claim the secrets
Make them known

After all the flowers have been offered, each person may reach into the cauldron and take out a stone or paper. The dance continues until all have chosen, but no one should look at what virtue they have chosen until the dance is finished. That can wait for later, either while sharing a ritual feast or even once you've left the circle.

No one should reveal to anyone else what is written on the stone or paper. This is your own personal exploration and no one else can or should tell you how to read it or react to it or enact it. You must decide the meaning of what the word means and how you're going to pursue it. If you're not quite sure, you can do some divination on it or ask for a sign.

You should also decide how much time you're going to dedicate towards instilling this virtue into your normal life. You could choose a short amount of time, such as a week or a month, or you might want to dedicate the traditional year and a day. Perhaps, once you've begun this exploration, you might end up with it becoming a part of you or decide that, well, you've tried it but it really isn't part of who you are or where you are going.

Use as many or as few words/virtues as you like. You can use the list below as a starting point.

Artistry
Admiration
Acceptance
Apology

Boldness
Beauty
Bravery
Brilliance
Balance
Bliss

Charm
Candor
Courage
Clarity
Compassion
Courtesy

Diligence
Daring
Discourse
Dignity
Desire
Directness

Endurance
Enigma
Eagerness
Ease
Earnestness

Faith
Focus
Fellowship
Fairness

Generosity
Grace
Gratitude
Gentleness

Hope
Honor
Humility
Happiness
Honesty

Imagination

Joy

Knowledge

Levity
Lightness
Light

Mirth
Mindfulness

Optimism
Openness
Originality

Peace
Pleasure
Passion

Perseverance

Perspective
Power

Quality
Quietude

Respect
Reverence
Risk

Sanctity
Serenity
Strength
Sweetness

Sensibility
Sensuality

Understanding   Verve   Wonder
Uniqueness   Validity   Wildness
Usefulness   Valor
                    Value
                    Vision
                    Vitality
                    Vigilance

Youth   Zest

Transformation Rite

When it comes to doing rituals for Cerridwen, She asks us to *"wear black if you must wear anything at all. No jewelry, no adornment. No paint upon your face. Nothing which is not of you. This is not plainness nor lack of vanity, but a promise to endure, to seek out all that remains when what is not is taken away.*

To understand beauty you must comprehend its lack, as to understand strength you must at times fail. Then you shall recognize what is most beautiful within you, that which is truly of you, and so come to strength, the strength born of doing what is right. Not the right of law or custom, but the right of the Old Gods of fate and knowledge. Of what is and what should yet be."

For this ritual, as for all rituals of Cerridwen requiring a cauldron of some kind, if you don't have one you can make do with a black bowl, but an actual iron cauldron or cooking pot is preferable if you can acquire one. You can sometimes find them at antique stores, but if you put water in the cauldron, be sure to dry it thoroughly afterwards and it might be a good idea to oil it on a regular basis to keep the surface from rusting.

Cast a circle as you normally would.

Place the cauldron in the center of the floor, moving the altar to the North of the circle if necessary. Conversely, you can also choose to put the cauldron on the altar. Set a tall glass enclosed candle (a seven hour candle can be acquired at many occult stores) in the center of the cauldron or use a tall candleholder. Pour water into the cauldron, an inch or so will do. Light the candle. It should be the only source of illumination in the circle.

Everyone holds an unlit candle and focuses on the central flame as the Priest, Priestess or a chosen person says:

As of old
We gather close around the fire
The fire which is the first gift
Though not the last
To come from the stars
From fire we were born
As much as from the waters
And from the depths of the earth
Which gave us form

Each person steps forward and drops something into the water in the cauldron, their offering—flower petals or seeds or small bones (chicken bones will do). After giving the item, each lights their candle from the candle in the cauldron.

Those who offer flower petals or seeds can say:

We offer life

Those who offer small bones might say:

We offer death

All then say:

Mother Cerridwen
We call
By the luck of three
By the three that fall
Blood to breath
And breath to speak
To name to know
To feel to be
Unlock our hearts
Unbind our souls
Hear us

For we shall not falter
Upon this path once begun
For we shall dare the flames
We shall dare the waters
The edge of all

Someone chosen or the Priest or Priestess goes to the North and lights the North candle, saying:

To the North

Repeat to the South:

To the South

Go to the East:

To the East

Finish in the West:

To the West

Everyone holds their candles in the middle, out over the cauldron and says:

Our light stands within
The dark shall not persuade us

All hold their own candles close to them, saying:

We shall persuade the dark

All blow out their candles and someone chosen says or the words may be shared or said by all:

To die to be born
A second time
The price of transformation
Is ours to pay
Ours to claim
We will not fear
Not within the circle
Of our hearts
And so we shall not forget
Not so long as life abides
Not so long
As death remains

All begin to slowly turn around the altar or the cauldron on the floor, saying:

Cerridwen
Mother
Show us the way
Show us the way

Continue to slowly circle the cauldron, half the people chanting quietly:

Go within

While the other half softly chant:

Cerridwen

Dance until the time is right, when all should slowly sink down to sit or lie on the floor, staring into the flame of the candle in the cauldron. At this point, everyone should seek a vision from the Goddess. Continue to stare into the flame or close your eyes, whichever way is most conducive to relaxation and opening yourself up. The chant may be continued through this or allowed to taper off naturally.

When all are finished and have received a message or a vision, they should re-light their candle from the cauldron candle and stand briefly in a circle together.

One at a time, everyone can say, or all can say together:

> **This I am**
> **And I am this**
> **A light amidst the darkness**
> **Wick and wax for the Gods**
> **A flame to see**
> **To burn**
> **To know**
> **All I am**
> **All I may yet be**

Feast together if you desire and share your visions if you feel comfortable doing so. You shouldn't share everything about your vision, though. The vision is part of your power and you mustn't give it all away. Always keep some aspect of the vision to yourself, whichever portion of it seems the most personal to you, the one you might feel rather reluctant to share.

Close the circle at this point and take your candle home with you. Burn it on the three nights surrounding the full moon—the day before, the day of, and the day after. Burn the candle until it's all gone.

Crown of Cerridwen Rite

Place the cauldron or a black bowl on the altar, surrounded by three or four candleholders. You will need a white candle, a black candle, and a red candle. If you choose to use four candleholders, then the fourth candle you have should be gold. If you don't use a golden candle, then you should have some golden thread or yarn.

You should also have some other pieces of yarn, red, black, and white, along with any beads or tokens—preferably gold in color—that you will bless during this rite and make into braids that you can wear. The length of the yarn will depend on what you intend to do with it, whether make them into bracelets or anklets or necklaces or simply lengths of yarn to keep on your own personal altar or by your bed.

Draw a circle as usual.

Have someone pour water or clear spirits into the bowl or cauldron, saying:

> **As the cup holds the future**
> **The cauldron**
> **The vision from which all springs**
> **Life and death**
> **The secret gift**
> **That exists within us all**
> **So we must choose to drink**
> **Each of us choose**
> **To live**
> **And to die**
> **To share of our secret self**
> **Our gift**
> **Our dream**

Dress each candle, spreading scented oil on it (you can use Venus oil made from Venus incense or any oil which appeals to you). Dress the black candle first, then the white, red, and finally the gold. This can be done by one person, or each person may help with dressing the candles.

As you dress the candles you may say, or say over them all once done:

> To give without fear
> And hesitation
> Without doubt or expectation
> What we see
> Within the cauldron
> What we taste
> Within the cup
> Must come to its fruition
> To awaken
> And rise
> A flame upon the wind

Place the pieces of yarn around the bowl or cauldron, along with any beads or tokens you intend to use, saying:

> By the twisted rope
> The scarlet milk-white braid
> Of fire and of frost
> The black depths
> We dare to drink
> To dream to see
> To be
> And to live to die
> So to learn to live again
> No more shadows
> But the light itself supreme

Set the candles in their holders and place them around the cauldron, one to each direction. Hold out your hands, kneeling around the altar or the cauldron, saying:

> **Lady of the deeps**
> **And the heights**
> **The scarlet**
> **The spark**
> **The stir of the spell**
> **The wave on the shore**
> **The shiver**
> **The spiral**
> **Deep and deeper to go**
> **Cerridwen**
> **Mighty Queen**
> **Through all that changes**
> **Show us**
> **Show us**
> **What remains**
> **Show us what always remains**

Light the first candle, the black candle, saying:

> **This we light in your name**

Light the second candle, the white candle, saying:

> **This we light in our own**

Light the third candle, the red candle.

> **This we light**
> **To show the way**
> **To illuminate the secret door**
> **The star of the sea**
> **The serpent horn**

You may then light the golden candle or wind the golden cord or yarn around the other three candles, linking them together and enclosing the bowl or cauldron.

You say or each person says in turn:

> **I pledge myself to vision**
> **To trust what is revealed**
> **I pledge myself to truth**
> **To face what lies concealed**
> **To take full hold**
> **Of the light**
> **And dare to face the dark**
> **To stand beneath**
> **The crown**
> **Set upon the open heart**

Stir the liquid in the cauldron slowly, always in groups of three—three stirs, six, nine, or twelve will do, saying as you do:

> **All that is, was**
> **All that was, will be**
> **All that will be, is**
> **Three in one**
> **And the one the crown of all**
> **An unbroken circle**
> **Where the light casts**
> **The shadow of life**
> **And death**
> **Is but a door**
> **To worlds as yet unknown**

Or you can say this in its entirety once, then simply repeat as you stir:

All that is, was
All that was, will be
Al that will be, is

Braid the pieces of yarn, attaching the beads or tokens if desired. If possible, wear what you have woven, but if you can't wear it all the time, at least wear it in ritual or whenever you are doing scrying or other sorts of divination. The rest of the time, you can keep the braid on your altar or near your bed.

This pledge can be for a month—from one full moon to the next—or whatever length of time you feel is appropriate. A year and a day is always a good idea, but perhaps making use of shorter lengths of time first would be a good way to gear yourself up for the prospect. You can, of course, pledge yourself to this for your entire lifetime.

Invocation of Cerridwen

This can be used to invoke Cerridwen into the ritual or into a Priestess so the Goddess can speak. If invoking into a Priestess, have her stand with her hands crossed over her chest, her head bowed. The cauldron can be set at her feet with saltwater in it. If desired, a floating candle can be placed in the water or a tall glass-enclosed candle.

Invoke with wand or bolene, saying:

> **Dark mother**
> **Bright mother**
> **You who keep the cauldron**
> **You who are the cauldron**
> **Of storms and tides**
> **Relentless and sure**
> **Where mystery abides**
> **And in abiding**
> **Is born and dies**
> **By the sharp and merciful blade**
> **Which severs the shade**
> **By the burning drink**
> **The food of Gods**
> **And damned mortals alike**
> **One word**
> **One word**
> **One spell**
> **One dream unfolding**
> **Each to the end**
> **And there to begin again**
> **Cerridwen**
> **Hear us**
> **Answer our call**
> **Bright mother**

Dark mother
Hear us
Be with us

Symbols of Cerridwen

A cauldron, of course, is the premier symbol of Cerridwen, preferably a black iron cauldron, one that you can fill with salt water or simply set a candle inside. Also, a greyhound or a hare, a hawk and a bird, an otter and fish, a hen and seed, or a statue of the Goddess Herself. A snake formed into a circle, biting its own tail, can also be used. Other symbols include a black scrying bowl or mirror, a small silver crown, and silver and gold candles. A piece of meteorite rock, if one can be obtained, or a piece of stone from a cave is also good. White feathers can also be used or a small image of a white sow.

"My cloak conceals the fire within. I stand upon the shores of the unknown uncertainty, the realms of within where mystery abides, the realm of self, ever in transformation. The animal shapes are but metaphors for the powers within, each a step and each a lesson, until at last you achieve the perfect seed—that which shall give birth to self.

Shhh…listen…do you hear the whisper? That's how it first comes. Pray that you hear it, that you heed it, that stronger measures are not called for. For the mercy of the Gods is a strange thing.

The mercy of the Gods is not for you to measure. Instead, it is we who measure, just as it is we who cut and we who weave. But don't worry, we are all in this together and so we know what it is to be measured, to be cut, to be woven. We know what it is to lose and be lost. We know for we are those who remember and so we are yet your kin in that. Brother and sister to your pain, we who first heard the whisper, who understood the quality of our name.

Drink and be drunk from. Do not seek to break the cycle, for that is beyond you all, though there are always those who think they are beyond the all and would seek ending for the sake of claiming they have power over all. But they do not. The only world they end is their own.

Look within the circle of the cauldron. What do you see? What do you not see? What sees you? Men have lost the knack of dreaming, imagining that it is only dreaming. But the first gift of the cauldron comes always in a dream, a dream of what may be. A dream of truth, a truth impossible to hold but not impossible to be. You choose, then, to chase the dream or to turn away. One is the way of transformation, from death to life and from life to death, while the other leads to the only true death there is—the fading away of all you are or ever were meant to be. To the blackness between, where even the light is utterly consumed.

When you refuse life, my cauldron, you eat yourselves."

Cerridwen

Part Three
Ariadne

Mistress of Spiders

Weave and weave
A web reveals
Stars hang down
Jewels and dreams caught and splendid
The spider mistress
Caresses them all in turn
Though she shall not keep them
For her own
Instead they belong to those
Who brave the way
Who follow the path
The shining road
Between this world and the next.

Milky-white
Red to blood
Eyes blink peacock-gleam
A blackened mirror of night reclaims
As vision reaches out
Always a reflection of who you are
Of what is needed
Of how it was always meant to be.

The grey ones
Only come when they are called
By the gracious Queen of Dread
Though She is more beautiful
Than any other
The lady of the sleeping lake
The same door
Which leads to the restless dead
As blood they know and to blood they go
The rushing horde

Her hounds
Her hands
Gentle on the binding rope
Stronger than any mere mortal man
Hands to wield the blade.

What is truth She asks
What is life she demands
Life and truth lies gilded by the light
The same fire which gave the Gods life
The fire of what is right
And real and strange
Glimmering within the
Golden words of the prophets
Of oracles and poets
As they lie transfixed by joy
By what their own words revealed.

Pain and ecstasy
She waits
Not the one who made the web
But the one who first walked it
And made a song of its threads
Who inspired others to sing
To seek the jewels
Which lie embedded in the maze
The pattern of the stars
The rhythm of the heart
The mystery of acknowledgment
Without which nothing
Could be known.

Though mystery remains
As ever
The spaces between the stars
The echo between the web

148

The light which casts the shadow
For as the more we come to know
The greater still it grows.

Night has fallen, the shadows taking refuge near the entrance to the underground, the Underworld. Light flares and spits in the dark as first one torch and then a second is lit by the wide, round mouth of the cavern set within the rocks at the edge of the sea. She moves as though in a trance, as though dancing, bare foot upon jagged stones and seemingly uncaring.

She wears a mask of polished copper and it catches the light as She turns and stands directly before the entrance. When She moves, the shadows cast by the torches twist, making the mask look first like an animal, wild and furious, and then the face of a woman beautiful enough to kill or die for. Black hair spills down around Her shoulders in tender ringlets, hair as dark as Her eyes.

She is a Princess, a Priestess, a Queen, a Goddess. Her dress betrays who She is, a red dress the same color as fresh blood. The hem of Her dress and Her belt is spun of golden thread and the spider that fashioned it hangs loosely off one end, a great golden and black spider with eyes like a thousand nightmares, a hundred thousand dreams. She is not the spider, but She knows well the spider's work.

She spreads Her arms and light weaves between Her fingers, taking form but not form, a red web, a golden spiral, a mystery, a puzzle. Not a puzzle that you can just figure out, but one that you must walk in order to seek out the secret that lies at its heart. It's a map of the maze, the tidal pull of the labyrinth, sea currents and underground rivers, the veins of the Earth.

"You can't find what you seek, unless you know what you seek," She says and puts Her hands back together.

When She opens them again it's to reveal a curved blade, a sacrificial knife. She studies it carefully, the torchlight catching along its length as She turns it this way and that. It's a plain blade, serviceable. No jewels or gold, but more than sharp enough to be the measure of mercy.

"Why the double edge?" She asks. "Why life? Why death? If you don't know the answer to that then you know nothing. Yet…the secret is to know nothing. Only then can you begin."

She raises the blade in a salute to the moon and, as She does, the white crest of the waves upon the rocks gives rise to a great bull of the sea. He emerges slowly, taking form as he leaves the waves behind. The moon stands briefly between his horns as he pauses, half in this world and half again in another. His eyes are black at first, then green, and finally warm gold, the eyes of beast or of a God. The mark of the Sea Gods is upon him, the sign of his willing life and gift.

"What the sea offers is not so easily ignored," She says. "The Minotaur was less monster than amalgam. Beast, man, God, monster, how many names do you prefer? Knowing that none of them are correct."

She lowers the knife and the bull bows down deeply before Her, only to rise again as a man, a man clothed in the moon and sea foam hide of the bull, his pale-gold hair long and tangled. He steps forward to meet Her, despite the blade. He holds himself proudly, the pulse in his neck steady and strong. No mere sacrifice then, but a willing one; the best of all sacrifices and the most sure.

"Who is the God within?" She asks, smiling ever so slightly. "I'm not a Goddess of pleasantries, but I'll tell you this much—don't ever stop and don't ever look back. Bad things happen to those who look back. A pillar of salt has nothing on what can happen."

150

The bull-man walks past Her, through the gateway of the torches, and into darkness. He disappears within, for it is there that he lives. After he has gone, She kneels down and sets the blade across the entrance, balanced between light and shadow, one edge in and one edge out.

"This bridge you know," She breathes. "But will you to leap? Will you dare? For those who do not, cannot say and those who do, will not speak."

She stands and, as She does, the mask slips free. It smashes on the rocks below, a million sharp shards and all of them reflecting the unknown.

The Labyrinth and the Leap of Ecstasy

The waves imprint the moon
Crescent hooves swift and sure
The ground will never be the same
Where he has walked
A crown half gold and half black
A face half kind and half cold
The beast king rules
What can never be tamed
From the sea he comes
The shaker of men's souls
Ancient stones tumbled down
To reveal the secret dark
Her hair tumbled down
As she bends to the waves
Blood trailing from the blade
The beast-king calls from below
Don't give him your name

Red thread, the blood price, spiraling down and around to meet the monster, he who guards the power within the puzzle and the good straight path of return. Red thread and golden, the path of the sun, the light hidden in flesh, the maze is a castle, a wheel, a spiral, and Ariadne holds the key to them all. Ecstasy is Her consort, the God of wine and blood, and like Him, Her way leads inwards as much as outwards, for you must lose yourself to gain yourself.

The labyrinth has been imagined as many things—the Underworld, a cave, a tomb, a dance, the road the dead must travel in their going in and their coming out. It can also be seen as a web, one comparable to the golden net of Aphrodite, Ariadne's sister-self. One of Ariadne's titles is *Mistress of Spiders* and so the labyrinth is spun, the great spider who creates it also known of old as Dread Fate.

The entrance to the cave is marked by two lit torches, not so much to give off enough light to see by, but to provide the way to the world of the serpentine labyrinth, the underground rivers of the Earth where water has carved out passage to the dark heart of the Mother. Water flows and as it flows it changes what it touches; even stone and mountains must yield before it.

The opening yawns black and cool, damp air pouring out, the arcane breath of the depths. Ariadne stands between the two torches, pale serpents twined upon Her bare arms, black ringlets of hair echoing the twists of the snakes She holds and the secrets of the maze behind Her. She does not offer those who come a mere spool of red thread, but the knowledge that the thread they seek to spin out behind them as they traverse the labyrinth is emblem of their lives and of their blood.

The snake twists and turns like water spirals, creating the ancient *meander*, a figure related to the maze. The serpent is symbol of the eternal cycle of life and death. When we are born here, we die in the land of death, and as we die here, we are born into that realm. The transition points are reflective of each other, mirrors in the Veil which separates the two worlds from each other—not just one snake biting its own tail, but two, thus creating the symbol of eternity, the figure "8" laid on its side.

All start here, at the gateway where the Goddess waits, expressionless and serene, Her dark eyes burning. Deep within the labyrinth, the God also waits, the God who wears the face of deepest nightmare and greatest aspiration. Yet, in this place, the God and the Goddess are as one, for to reach the center of the maze is also to reach the edge of the Void. The same as to go beyond the edge of the Abyss is to find yourself back at the beginning point.

The story of Ariadne is one of love and betrayal. The Princess, Ariadne, was the daughter of King Minos of Crete and his lovely Queen, Pasiphae. Pasiphae was also mother to the Minotaur, making Ariadne and the dread man-bull half brother and sister. In retribution for a broken oath from King Minos, Poseidon made his wife fall in lust with a beautiful white bull—the bull which was originally a gift from the God of the Sea—and from this union sprang the monster, half-man and half-bull. The labyrinth was built to house him and he was fed by the tribute price of Greek youth, seven men and seven women each year.

In the tale that has come down to us, Ariadne fell in love with the Greek hero, Theseus, who came to try to stop the tribute and slay the beast relentlessly consuming his kin. The princess ended up betraying her father, her people, her country, all in the name of that love. She gave this handsome foreigner the thread needed to solve the riddle of the labyrinth and to get away with killing the Minotaur. After which, she sailed away with her beloved, only to end up abandoned by him on the island of Naxos.

All of which certainly puts Ariadne in a bad light as well as Theseus, a supposed hero and all around good guy. This makes very little sense on the surface of things. So it should come as no real surprise that this story is but an overlay on a far more ancient tale, one where Ariadne wasn't just some princess. She is a Goddess and Her consort is Dionysus, the lord of dance, drink, drama, and ecstasy. He is also a God of the Sea and of the sacred bulls of the sea. This makes Ariadne a princess, Queen, priestess, and instrument of merciful death. While Her love and lover, Dionysus, is the sacrifice, the bull who is King and fool, the dance of life and death that is also the play.

The later version of the story is one of a hero and of the defeat of a monster in the dark. It's the story of the love between a hero and a princess and of her eventual abandonment. Not much of an up-lifting tale; a woman who betrays her people and position and a hero who takes advantage of that love and trust and uses it to his own ends. But the story behind the story is the one that counts, the one that makes sense. The hero goes into the labyrinth, there to face the beast, who was born of the Gods and thus represents Divine power.

The father of the Minotaur was a white bull, gift of the Sea God, and his mother a Queen; he could claim to share in both the fertile and ultimately sacrificial nature of true Kings, of what they are born to be and to do. Minotaur means the *taur* or bull of Minos, the Lord of Crete and clearly was a symbol of his authority and vigor. Not only did this power have to be fed, but it needed to be protected. As the Minotaur went, so went the King and as the King went, so went Crete. The human-Divine man-bull was the Kingship fully realized.

The struggle of Theseus, the young hero, was to teach him about his own true nature and about the cycle of life, death, and rebirth that he is not only a part of, but to be representative of. He becomes King in the process, he becomes Dionysus, the chosen ecstasy of sacrifice, and takes as his bride the princess, the priestess, who becomes Queen to his King. She is a not a priestess of Dionysus, one of the Maenads who consume and are consumed by their God, but His consort and equal, half of an ancient couple far older than the Greek twist on Their story.

As Ariadne says *"Theseus was a fool, a sacred fool. All fools are sacred for they do what others say they cannot. They do not care. Instead, they dare. Daring is what makes the possible impossible and the inevitable, unlikely. Most would say it is the art of possibility, for in daring you can make anything happen, but it is more than that. That is only the outward sign, the simple magick. It is easy to make impossibility, possible. It is far more difficult to make the possible, impossible—or is it?*

I do not make the rules of the world, the rules that you all choose to live by. I am not about rules. Rules are just ways of saying no, no, no, when I am all about the yes. Theseus was all about the yes. He did not care. Death was not his enemy, but his challenge. Fools always go for the challenge. It did not matter what waited and watched for him there in the dark, in the dank, in the cold. It mattered that he went willingly into darkness and let the darkness eat him up. A monster, as you put it, would either arise from this or a genius. Not a genius as you think of one today, but the sacred fool turned king. There are all sorts of genius and his was not that of the mind, but of the heart.

Theseus walked the path of blood, stole the horns of the God, and became that which he was all along. Do you not know his name now? What other sacred king wears horns and comes from the waves? The sacred fool is always an actor, though what hides behind the mask is always the same. He was the dance long before he was the vine. He has always been the feast, the fool, the king, nameless and unnamed. Men do not always know they play the fool, not until the madness comes, and then it is too late."

It makes sense that Ariadne's beloved would be a God who also embodies the Arts, particularly the poetry and drama of the play. They are tied together by the emotional intensity evoked by taking part in the act of creation, and by the spark, flash, and charge that gives that creation life. Drama wears a mask to become someone or something else, embodying the passion of the story and creating the connection between the audience and the spirits that the actors— the Priests and Priestess of the Art—stand in for during the telling of the tale. The act upon the stage is a reflection of life, the play we act in, the game that we play.

Dionysus's Maenads belonged as much to Muse as they did to Him. They were inspired to partake of the drama of worship and lose themselves in madness, a madness that imparts a direct and unequivocal experience of the Divine, of the great web. The same web that cannot be touched, unless you have entered an altered state, sometimes akin to madness. This is one of the gifts of the Gods, imparted by Their embrace, for They are capable of standing far closer to the blinding light of the All than we.

Ariadne tells us *"there was no Theseus. It was always the God. The bullman was always the God. The feast was always the God, and the drink of the feast. To leap the bull was to dance the God's dance. Just because a God is nameless does not mean He does not take on names. He 'abandoned' the woman on an island, and an island is always death. Black sails—he sailed with death. They wanted their kind to be lord of death and of life alike, to have defeated the God, to be a God. The ships of Dionysus always sailed with black sails. They were tidings of the coming storm."*

The Maenads ran with this storm in their hearts, wild women, enchanted by the blood of their God, their beloved and their beast. They ran with the grace of the Divine, as much a force of nature as the wind and the waves, one with the power of the Muse. They partook of blood and they gave of blood, both their own and that of the vine, and they lived the play. They walked the labyrinth within them, ecstatic creatures, mad, powerful, unstoppable, filled to the brim and beyond with the rapture of the universe.

We seek that ecstasy, that experience, the touch of the Divine. Yet, just as the Maenads had to eventually come down from their high, we can't hold onto that place all the time. Still, once we have succeeded in achieving it, even though the memory will lose its clarity no matter how hard we try to keep hold of it, we can still retain some small portion of what we have seen and felt. Certainly, we can keep hold of enough to know how badly we want it again.

To pursue the inspiration of the Muse is like pursuing the connection to the wild Divine represented by Dionysus. When we feel the pleasure, the joy, the satisfaction of having that energy pour through us, we long to have it happen again and again. We ache to find ourselves tapping into that flow of energy, feeling it rushing through us, filling all that we create. We long to look at what's been created and be proud of the part we played in its birth.

When writers lie in the arms of the Muse, the words just flow, sometimes so quickly it's a struggle to keep up. Yet the words are good words, right and powerful and beautiful, even perfect at times. Reading them later, once the charge has dimmed, the writer often marvels—could I have written that? The same goes for painting, acting, healing, dancing, cooking, driving a car, or even giving advice or saying the right thing at just the right time.

Anything done well, anything done *marvelously* well, that is created in and by and through bliss, is an Art blessed by the Muse. Sure, it's typical to think of the Arts as writing or painting or dancing, rather than seeing it in all aspects of our lives. But as we all have different interests and talents, different callings, different ways of seeing, whatever form our bliss takes, therein lies our Art.

Spiders weave a part of themselves into their webs. The webs are both purpose and artistry, beauty and strength. Water drops caught in the web glimmer and break into rainbow light, crystals capturing the light of the rising and setting sun and, more subtle still, that of the changeable moon. In the same way, we weave parts of ourselves into our dreams, into our rising and falling, our lives and deaths, our own changeable masks. We weave our Art and are woven by it.

Ariadne is mistress of all who weave. What is woven is not just silken thread, but lives, stories, dreams, and visions. The web extends out from a central point, touching everything, expanding further and further until it reaches the outermost boundary of what is known. It expands until all that remains without is the great unknown. This is where the real exploration, the true mystical and cunning journey, begins at the last.

Mazes take us on journeys. They lead us deep into the mystery of our own being, just as they can take us to other worlds, to the Otherworld, the land of the Gods, and of the ancestors. Like the dance, mazes can put us into a trance state and they can wake us up.

They are a means of traveling without traveling—not the straight path, but the winding road, the spiral of time and transformation, the snake's twist that combines beginnings and endings.

Between the silver gate of the moon and the golden door of the sun, the world lies held like a precious egg. Around the circumference of the all coils the great world-snake, the one who laid the egg. Everything we know and don't know is but a shadow cast by the light of the Source, and that light comes through the sun in both visible and invisible ways, in Light and in Love. Those who worship the Sun really worship this Source which creation is the mirror-reflection of.

As the stars are the children of the light and the dark, we are also dual in nature. Our parents are Mother Earth and the Lord of the Sky, the Sun. The stars that swirl and spiral are our as yet unborn Brothers and Sisters. We can rightly say we stand with a foot in two worlds, the earth and the sky, night and day, life and death. Witches and cunning folk of all kinds are born to bridge that gap. We carry currents of energy from one side to another, to keep a dynamic balance, having traversed the labyrinth not just once, but many times.

When we pierce the heart of the labyrinth, we grasp that single point. It's there we can see who we really are, as we look full-on into the perfect mirror, the one sometimes symbolized by a still pool or a well or a bowl. When we look into the well, into the mirror, we see exactly who we are and why we are here. We know our place in the tapestry, what our thread is meant to touch and to tie together. There, we may become the world and see not just into our heart, but the heart of mystery itself.

Ariadne says *"mazes are mother to the trance, the same trance that men dance to achieve. The maze and the dance thus share an equal place in the hearts of men, one a way of the earth and one of fire. The trance itself is where they are met in the middle, a meeting that precipitates the maelstrom, the firestorm, the raging current which surrounds the eye of peace.*

We dance and, in dancing, we spin. We walk the maze and in walking, we are lost. To spin and be lost to the spinning is to seduce the maelstrom, to seek out the storm of fire, sinking ever downwards through both until at the last the heart of both is achieved, the heart which is also an eye.

You thought it was a coincidence that the tornado, the hurricane, the storm has an eye? There are no coincidences..."

In the eye of the storm, in the center of the labyrinth lives the Minotaur, a creature that is half-man and half-bull, half-mortal and half-divine. It's not surprising that he is part bull, for the bull was sacred in many pagan religions and a favored sacrificial animal. This is a concept which goes all the way back to the Apis bulls of ancient Egypt, where one of the titles of Pharaoh included the "Bull of Heaven." The God Dionysus is also a horned God of goats and bulls, consort to Ariadne, and He was often made sacrifice to his own followers.

Cows were related to Hathor, the Goddess of love and death, as well as Hera, the Queen of the Gods. Cows are givers of milk and figure in many creation myths. Even the Milky Way is named after droplets of sacred milk as they spill across the vast night sky. We may not think that comparing a woman to a cow is a nice thing to say today, but in ancient times it would have been a high compliment.

The Minotaur is the God-force, the sun, the storm, fertility and sacrifice. He lives in a maze that is the womb of the earth from which all are born and reborn. He is the mystery at the center of the maze, guardian of the treasure and the treasure itself. He is the infamous and dangerous Guardian at the Gate. When we dare the Minotaur in his lair, we take back our own power. We reclaim our energy and heritage—the fire of the Sun, the fire in the blood and in the marrow of the bone, the gift and promise of the Gods.

The unwinding of the thread, means letting go in order to descend into the labyrinth. We go into the ground of our selves and there face that which keeps our power chained up. This is the chain that must be broken, the Minotaur defeated and devoured. We don't do this to kill him, but to claim his power, the power that is our own power. Then, when we find our way back out of the dark afterwards, back into the world above, we emerge with a greater light, with the treasure from beneath the hill.

The golden treasure is the fire of the Sun and the invisible aspect of the Sun, the essence of Love. What we reclaim from the maze is an understanding of that power. Once we can grasp it, we can touch it within ourselves and within others, whose hearts are open to it. This pure life force cannot be denied nor bound nor destroyed, though we can sometimes attempt to cut ourselves off from it.

This is a fatal mistake, one born of doubt and fear. The Minotaur will use this fear to terrify us, taking on the forms and face of what scares us. The face of fear takes its cue from the seeker just as the means to defeat those fears will also take on the form that is required. Only once this has been done and the monster "destroyed," can we be reborn to a second life. Only then can we come back with an understanding of the fire in our hearts and the ability to use that fire in our lives, magick, and the Arts.

Every life is a labyrinth and every death a maze. They overlap, as the realms of life and of death overlap, mirroring each other. We must all learn to walk the maze of self before we can walk the greater maze. We have to unravel and re-weave our own lives before daring to unravel the cords that bind the universe together and face what lies behind the mask.

One way to walk the maze is by courting ecstasy, for the unbinding of the senses can take us to the center. But, before that, we have to first create a foundation, an anchor, a home; otherwise we risk becoming lost in the riddle, in the darkness, easy prey to the monster. We might not be able to find our way back again without that bright spark, the one thing that is ours and only ours.

The mazes we walk take on many forms and may even change as we walk—from a cave to a web to a riddle to a tomb—but no matter how it appears it involves a birth. This birth from darkness is similar to the birth that's commemorated each year at the Winter Solstice. At that time, we welcome not just the return of the Sun or the birth of the god of the Sun, but the very idea of birth, of the return. We celebrate the child as something bright and new coming into the world.

This rebirth is the star that shines brighter than any other, that shines only for our eyes, an omen of the open door. To bind the light to the bone, to make it real in the here and now, real upon the Earth...for that reason we venture into the maze, into death, and seek out the light and the life buried there. We go below the mountain to where the power of Gods and Kings waits.

This is the riddle of the story made manifest. Our lives include blind twists and turns, no certainty of destination, and equally no surety of return once we find it. It's filled with the ever-present potential of danger and of wonder. To walk the maze is to go on a spiritual journey, yet it's also living our life to the utmost. Just as when we meet other people along the way, those who aid us and who present challenges, they are as much reflections of our own inner being as they are people on their own unique journey.

Through the medium of the Arts we can manifest beauty in all its aspects, even beauty that is so incredible, so powerful, so vivid that it's terrifying. Through the Arts we can manifest Truth, Wisdom, Liberty, and other concepts and ideas that normally are much too great to come into our world as they are. The Arts are one of our best tools for creating change, for providing illumination, and for accessing those lost and forgotten parts of ourselves and the world that shouldn't have been lost or forgotten.

Once we've manifested inspiration in some form, brought it to birth and granted it a life of its own, we can never take back again and never reclaim it. Accordingly, if we cannot give freely—without expectation of recompense—then we shouldn't give at all because what we've created is a gift to the world. Any benefit we may derive from it is no different than anyone else's chance of benefit. It no longer matters that we were parent to the manifestation of the idea. Pure and simple, we can't own it.

We might own the painting or the words on the page, but we can't restrict the idea that the words or the paint reveals. We can't bind revelation or vision. Certainly, we can't control the feeling that the painting or the book or the movie or the song evokes in someone else. What we have provided is the medium. It remains for others to look inside and walk away with that certain special something, the potential for understanding or for transformation.

Ariadne tells us to *"love what you create and what you create shall be alive. It's as simple as that. If you do not care, then they shall not feel, they can not be. Do not bring into being what you do not love, for we all know the folly of that. You see it all around you, the foolishness of men who create simply because they can and do not stop to ask the price. Unfeeling things, these creations, and do they have a soul? Do they?*

What do you think, you who made them and never loved them. You who thought the Gods were dead. It is not the Gods you must fear for, but man. The Gods do not die, but man does. Without love, what life? I am not a Goddess of soft petals and sweetest kisses, but even I know the truth of life. Even I must bow to love."

164

Ideas and inspiration come from elsewhere, but the only way that these ideas enter into our world is by the gift of form. This is under the auspices of the Muse—not the idea itself, unformed, unnamed, unknown—but the ability to touch the place where ideas are born. A dark and ancient and dreadful place, one more strange and dire and lovely than any number of words or quality of paint or any voice could ever fully convey; though, not for lack of trying.

When we connect to that place and work to bring something back, channeling its manifestation, we pay the price of the Art. Of course, there's the personal cost of time and energy, the sheer life-force that we call upon in order to bring it to being, but we also must pay the personal price of inner transformation in allowing the energies to flow through us. We must dare to create and dare to let go of what we create, allowing it to find its own way in the world, to unfold its own destiny.

Of course, how that idea first comes into being remains very much in our own hands, for as Ariadne says *"I have no poetry. I have only the truth. It is you who make poems of my truths."*

Within Darkness

Grape leaves and sacred ivy
Wind around a spiral horn
A circlet of stars
Crown the bridal veil
On bended knee he offers
His blood the wedding cup
They stand together
Stern and proud
Wild and unchained
No one could claim them
The bull and the bull's daughter
Father and mother
Sister and brother
Lovers upon the mountain
In dappled shadow
And honeyed madness
They taste each other
And we taste of them
Blood and honey
Wine and blossoms
Drifting in the sweet salt wind

Deeper and deeper into the dark, the thread unwinds; thread the color of blood and sacred madness, the color of kings. All is still here, the stone walls breathing out cool air. The voice of the Old Ones cries out from the depths, yet it is a silent cry for their language is the language of silence. They are the mystery in the quiet places, what cannot be spoken of save in quick flashes of direct understanding—one soul, one heart linked together.

The passageway spirals in and around and down. We descend near enough to touch the roots of the mountain, where ancient secrets yet remain unknown and unsaid, waiting for those who must come. What lies within our bones also exists within the depths of the earth. They share the past and we build upon them. We go back to the bone. Though, of course, this path is never entirely safe, for mystery is always dangerous and knowledge comes with a cost, especially knowledge of ourselves.

One way we share these gifts of the depths is through the Arts. We go into the darkness and come back with wild and wonderful images, dreams, visions, and aspirations. We have to go on then to give them grounding in this world. We have to grant them physical reality in whatever fashion we're best capable of. The ways that we do this are as varied as life itself.

Basically, the Arts can include anything that we are enthralled and enraptured by even as we do it. Those same Arts are capable of deeply touching and inspiring those around us. One way of looking at this is that anything that we do when we are "in the zone," or "in the groove," means that we have succeeded in tapping into the current of the Muse. If one is a writer, it may feel as though the words were there all along and you just have to get them down on paper. A musician might hear the music fully orchestrated in their head and a sculptor see the image as though already there, only trapped in stone.

What results is something that can stir people to tears, to laughter, and more than that—something which can alter their world, change perception, inspire action, awareness, and awakening. Some people call it having a certain special something extra, a touch of pixie even. It's what turns something good into something great, the average into the amazing, the ordinary into the outstanding. It's what makes magick.

Sure, it has to be something we're basically good at—talent does require practice, after all, to bring it to life—but more than that it must be what we love to do, what we will give up other things to do, what we are *compelled* to do. We are drawn back to it despite

168

normal needs and considerations like food and sleep. It should make us feel not just good, but powerful, so that even as we expend energy doing it, it energizes us at the same time. It fills us up, rather than draining us, despite all we put into it. It should fulfill us, making our hearts pound and our skin tingle.

This is the same road that Prometheus walked, that Icarus flew. It's searching for what lies beyond the known horizon...as we dream tomorrow's dreams, making fantasy come true. The rising star of the East foretells what may be, but only if we brave the maze, claim our hearts, and take up the challenge of infinite creation. We have to go into the West to come back around to the East, to be born with the dawn. Like the Sun, we go down into darkness and travel the dread realms before returning to the light, before realizing we are the light.

This power is our true birthright, but so few seek to claim it. Many settle instead for a lazy half-life half-death, narrow and restrictive. They fear to be free, remaining instead with what is assumed to be safe. But there is no safety, no surety, for without risk there is no life. Life is risk. We can't get around that. Just as we can't get around that we all *chose* that risk, chose to be here. We all decided to be born, knowing that what awaited were all the fears and uncertainties of the physical world. But we were also aware that there would be joys and pleasures, pleasures made all the more poignant by the fact that they don't last.

But we're not just here to undergo personal transformation, though that's part of where it takes us. We're also here to be a bridge between this world and another, the place where all is possible, and help bring to physicality that which has never been seen before. We open that door through the focus of our wills and through the sheer strength of our emotion.

What comes through that door passes through our spirits because our spirits never really leave the beginning place, at least not so long as a single, precious spark, a small and glimmering seed, remains intact within us. This spark can be nurtured into a bright flame, a star upon the Earth, opening the way for other lights, other stars to become real. It's part of our job to take on a body to experience the physicality of life and to help bring other spirits, other possibilities, dreams, ideas, and Divine fire, into the world of men.

When we shine, the fire within us shines. When we shine, what we create shines. This can make the world shine as it's meant to. We create Art and we are a part of the Art we create. Inspiration alone is not enough. We can be inspired all we like, but if we don't do the work to bring that inspiration to life, it won't exist here. To fully come into being, this inspiration must be linked to the active principle and be given physical expression.

All artists, including cunning folk and Witches, can serve as channels for these ideas, these gifts, in order to serve the work. It's no coincidence that the Craft is called a Magickal Art. It's meant to be pleasurable, joyful even, to bring powers into focus for transformation, healing, fertility, and a better life for the community and the world. A ritual without bliss, without inspiration, serves neither the Gods nor the practitioner. A proper ritual is a doorway to the beyond as much as any painting or book. It's a way for something unrealized to be realized and enter into existence.

Of course, to make that happen we have to choose the form. We have to have one vision in mind, not many different ones. Each individual Witch can, of course, affect their own channeling, but to work together to bring through something larger all must have a shared focus. Through this shared purpose, shared goals, shared resolve, we can work towards a blending of individual energies, powers, talents, and gifts in order to create a greater whole. Something far more than the sum of the parts and something with a life and consciousness all it's own. We don't have to lose our individuality, but become a bright star in a glimmering web of stars, part of a constellation.

170

However, desire—like any tool—must be attuned to purpose. It must be honed and sharpened; otherwise, it can be overwhelming. We require the peace at the center of the fire, the balance. This peace is the calm surety of the Goddess within the burning whirlwind of the God. This is the foundation for the tower we seek to build to touch the sky, for the bridge across worlds. It's the peaceful center formed from the torrent of unleashed madness.

Words can be not just words but windows, spells to make connections and to make things happen. Today, spells have come to mean specially charged words, motions, and objects that we have spent time and energy investing with intent and power; or objects and words that have come to us as having been filled with magickal energy. But, in the past, all words and writing and images were perceived as spells. Accordingly, any modern story, poem, movie, or image can become as a spell if enough energy is put into them.

There are countless numbers of characters in books and movies and on television, yet how many take hold of us in some way? How many books or movies have we not simply enjoyed, but found profound or stirring, with disturbing characters or scenes that made us think and, more importantly, make us *feel*. How many characters do we not only remember, but become fascinated by and actually form emotional attachments to as we come to like or dislike, love or hate them.

When we give a character that comes from the Muse their voice, we are tapping into a channel that not only can make words flow, but actually bring characters to life. Despite not having an actual physical form here in this world, they can still become real in a way and have an effect on material reality, even if only through the reaction other people have to them. These characters and what they go through during the story can reflect issues in the lives of physical people or in the group psyche, even a place.

Emotion finds expression through the Arts in the form of a manifestation of an underlying—sometimes otherwise inexpressible—idea or feeling. The book or movie or television show, the drama and the characters that live that drama, can become a touchstone for the energies of the Otherworld to enter our own. What's trying to be unfolded pours through the metaphor of the living character, a being that is partly here and partly there, the book or movie becoming a gateway.

People have always told stories and those stories have multiple layers of meaning and purpose. They didn't just serve to pass the time, but to hand down the culture to the next generation—morals, insights, hopes, fears, heroes and villains and what is expected of both, how a boy becomes a man and a girl, a woman. They tell us what the Gods want of us and what we should want of the Gods. What we should search for in life and discover in death. How the world first came into being and how we did.

Mythology seeks to tell the Great Story, a story that we all play a part in. It's not exactly the same as history, for it's not a collection of facts, figures, dates, names, and the theories that have spun off of them about what happened and what it means. We can't make a powerful story out of the pages of a historical tome, not without adding in "characters" that we can connect to and care about. Instead, we have to invoke the quality of drama; the nuances of the human heart, to make those once-living people live again, to believe that we know them.

For example, we can decide to read a history of the Scottish battle to be free of English rule, but how much more powerful was it when we sat down in a movie theatre to watch it brought to life through the medium of actors and action. We are inspired not just by what really happened back then, but by the emotional connections we make to the characters—historical or otherwise—who are living the moment before our eyes. We feel and so we touch what was, just as we can touch what will be.

Ariadne says: *"All things take on a life of their own as they are born into the world, though not all bear a physical form. Does that make them any less real, any less alive? Men have fought wars and died over such matters, over living ideas, deathless dreams. It is an insult to claim that you and only you know what is real. Real is always changing. It is never the same. Each moment to the next both creates and destroys. New worlds rise and old ones pass away, all in the blink of an eye.*

What you bring into the world is real, even though once it is here it changes and changes again, thus proving it is alive. No box can contain what the ancients spin, what the window of dreams brings into the world, what man wishes to life. Can you say with utter certainty what life is, when you cannot even understand death? To know one, you must know both. You must die to live again, and live with death upon your shoulder at all times, not just at the end."

Beings exist regardless if that existence is in the world of the living, the realm of the dead, or some other realm entirely. Imagining that everything must have a physical form in order to claim existence, is rather a narrow way of viewing the world. Simply because some beings don't currently have physical bodies here doesn't mean they're not "real." Reality has many layers, and what we can see and taste and touch and smell and hear is but one aspect; it's as though we could only see the color red and have come to think that a rainbow has only one color, because that's all we can comprehend it has. It doesn't mean that the other colors have gone away or never existed, simply that we don't have the capability to notice them.

In the same way, just because we cannot see or touch a physical body or hear a physical voice doesn't mean that there is a corresponding lack of reality. Beings may have many other sorts of "bodies," or even no body at all and still be alive and aware and capable of interacting with us. Some of these beings are characters that have sprung from the pages of a favorite book, movie, story, myth, play, or even a game. Sometimes, actors embody them for a time, so we can "see" them, and there are quite a few stories floating around where these same actors talk about having a "character" become way more than just a role, even of being able to talk to the character as they would to another person.

The same holds true for writers. Some authors will admit, openly or reluctantly, about having characters argue with them, refusing to do this or that, even sometimes going even further than that. One famous example of this is the Bronte sisters. They worked together on stories set in a particular universe and had the characters take on a life of their own, including one of them appearing briefly before their creator's startled eyes.

Ariadne tells us to *"love them and they shall come. What, you ask? Why, those to inhabit the shape you have spun for them. They are the wine within the cup, the blood within the flesh, the light within the stone. No more pretty words—they are the spirits drawn to the passion of creation, much as you were drawn to this life. In fact, exactly the same."*

The better the writer or the actor is at channeling this personality, this force, this being, the more powerfully they/it can come through and find expression here. The more pure the channel, the more true the "character" will be. And all the more likely that the channeling, the "character" will resound through society, taking on a momentum and personality all its own, sometimes going far beyond what the writer or actor originally had in mind.

The "characters" themselves, behind the personality, the living mask, are often stand-ins for greater powers or elements, consciousnesses that need to be damped down in order for us to interact with them. In this way, for example, an actor like Johnny Depp can become the physical means by which a greater or smaller aspect of the being known to us as Captain Jack Sparrow can walk in our world. While, Jack Sparrow is, himself, a living and conscious expression of a greater power known as Freedom.

174

All inventions, from the great to the small, have to come from somewhere, and to get to our world they need to find their way through the hands and voice of someone who lives here. These visions come in many different ways, from dreams to experiencing the *Eureka!* moment when an idea overwhelms us, a lightning bolt striking fire in our minds and bodies, leaving us shaking and inspired with the urge to do. It then takes talent and the experience gained from practice to help give this vision, this idea, a form.

But to do this we must choose to plunge into the current, giving ourselves over to it, not knowing where it will lead. Exciting and scary at the same time, this current comes with a rush of emotion and even physical sensation. We are exhilarated, breathless, in love with the idea and with the thought of giving it life. For throughout history we have loved ideas and longed to give birth to them, to make our dreams come true. To give them life and hope that they will continue on long after we have passed away.

Ariadne tells us to *"clothe what comes to you. Make it beautiful, make it bright, make it as great as you are able. Do not stint nor fear nor dally. Opportunity comes when it will and leaves swiftly. If you do not catch hold of it, who knows if it shall come again. Do not stint on yourself nor fear what you shall make nor delay overlong in the making of it. For if you do not catch hold, someone else may."*

Everyone has a dream. Everyone has a vision. They wait for us to take note of them, to offer them a way into this world. We all have a talent—at the very least one, if not more—to release, to touch, to know, to offer up to the world and to the future. We are not born empty-handed into life, but with the door to the power of the Divine inside us. It remains to us to seek the key and to swing it open; facing what comes afterwards with all our strength and compassion.

When we deny ourselves, our gifts, our talents, our dreams, who we really are deep down inside—we deny the world. We make it

175

less than what it could be, rather than more. When we run away from or deny our bliss, what makes us feel most alive, what inspires us to our very best—we deny the world. Each of us is here for a reason, even though we may have forgotten that reason.

We all have to do the work, though. We have to sit down in front of the keyboard or typewriter, set up the canvas and get the paints ready, practice scales or do spells and divination, whatever it takes to get going and show the universe that we are in a place to receive the bolt of inspiration. We have to hone the skills to bring it home, to build the framework for what's to come through. We must start with the talents that we've been given, choose which is our bliss, which appeals to us the most, and apply ourselves to it.

Preparation and intent provide the fertile ground for the seed that comes from elsewhere. Together, we of this world and the great powers create the ever-expanding universe. Through us, they are projected into the realm of the material. From the unknown, the unimaginable, to the known and imaginable—though the same mystery lies at the heart of it all, as it lies at the heart of each of us and always will.

A Prayer to Ariadne

By the web of stars and dreams
By the spinning and the spun
Destiny
Inspiration
As they meet within the darkness
And there create
The most blinding sword of light
The cup of praise
And the crowned heart
Which is the intersection
Of faith
And of fate
Sons and daughters of fortune
Blessed ones
We who have dared
To choose and to be chosen
To weave and to be woven
We who have answered the call
Of the priesthood
We beg a blessing for our Art
Oh glorious one
Lady of sea and storm
Of thorn and leaf
Rose and crown
Lover of the mad god
And of the wild hills
Where the ancients dance
Bestowing joy and despair
We beseech thee
Fill our cups
We who dare
And let our fate

Be as one with the heart
Of the immortal stars

Rite to Ask a Vision of Ariadne

Paint a maze or a spider web on a piece of cloth or heavy paper. The pattern should be large enough to accommodate a candleholder in the middle. Set the piece of cloth or paper on the floor or on an altar. Opposite you, place a mirror, either a free standing one or one that you can prop up on the back of a chair. Cover the mirror with a piece of dark cloth. This may be done in ritual or without ritual, though you may want to at least draw a circle before beginning.

Set up four candleholders to the West, East, North, and South. Light the West candle with a candle or tape and hold it up before you, saying:

> **To feel and to dare to feeling**
> **All life**
> **All death**
> **Is risk and renewal**
> **For all that we know**
> **We do not know all**

Light the North candle, saying:

> **To be and to know one's being**
> **The essence and the holy**
> **Names of the gods**
> **For all that we do**
> **Reflects who we are**

Light the East candle, saying:

> **To know and to act in knowledge**
> **The light that is born**
> **Shines forth in all directions**

179

For all that we dare
Will make the world

Light the South candle, saying:

To be strong and to do what must be done
Treading the path
Of silence and of mystery
For even eternity
May at last be altered

Light the candle set in the center of the pattern and say:

Vision
Belief
Desire
Transformation
The labyrinth is a mirror
And shows us
What we already know
What we already feel
What we already are
Leaving us to act in union
With the will of the divine
I am a servant of choice
A servant of change
One with the spider
One with the web

Ariadne
You who are mistress of spiders
Show me my power
Show me my place
The source of the fire
Which came down from the stars
And danced on the waters

Show me
The thread of my life
That which is woven into the very
Heart and secret and fabric
Of the maze

Uncover the mirror and gaze into its depths.

It is probably a good idea to have pen and paper at hand to write down what you see.

Afterwards, you might wish to make an offering to Ariadne for your vision, preferably by creating something to give to Her.

Blessing Rite of Ariadne

For this rite you will need a crown, one with seven stones (large rhinestones can be used) or stars on it. You can make the stars out of heavy paper and cover them with silver paint or even use star-shaped ornaments if you find something you like.

You also should have a spool of red thread or red cord.

Cast a circle as usual.

The Priest or Priestess or a chosen person says:

> **Black skies**
> **Black seas**
> **Lightning strikes**
> **The scarlet thread**
> **Hold fast**
> **Hold strong**
> **We stand upon the edge**
> **The sea below us**
> **The sky above**
> **Let the fire come down**
> **Let it dance among us**
> **Let it dance within**
> **To cry**
> **To wail**
> **The song of the ancients**
> **Bahk hai**
> **Bahk hai**

All join in, shouting:

> **Bahk hai**
> **Bahk hai**

Have the Priestess stand to the North with her hands crossed over her chest and her head bowed. She should be holding a bolene if you have one.

The Priest invokes, saying:

> **By the crown of the north**
> **The circle of the dead**
> **The crooked moon**
> **And the silver blade**
> **Come to us Ariadne**
> **Bless us**
> **We are not afraid**

The Priest sets the star crown on the head of the Priestess and everyone begins to chant softly, continuing until the Goddess appears:

> **Black skies**
> **Black seas**
> **Lightning strikes**
> **The scarlet thread**

When Ariadne is there, offer Her the red thread or cord. She may ask questions of you or simply bless your undertakings.

When you wish to dismiss Ariadne, simply remove the star crown and ask for the Priestss to return to you.

Threading the Maze Ritual

If you have a large enough space available, either indoors or outdoors, you can create a labyrinth to walk. Mazes have been formed out of hedges, turf, or raised lines of earth and some farmers today create mazes in their crops. For this work, you won't want to create a puzzle maze, one that you have to solve in order to get to the center, but a unicursal labyrinth, in which there is only one way to go.

You can create a maze by setting stones or cutting sod as was done in ancient times, but a quicker way today to construct one is by using string, rope, or baseball chalk. Chalk has the added bonus of disappearing with a good rain. In the wintertime, you can create a maze by trampling down snow into a pattern. For added visibility, several containers of a cheap, brightly colored drink mix can be poured along the path.

If you desire to walk a maze after dark, you can set four torches out along the perimeter or use the light of the full moon. Both are an eerie and illuminating experience, one where you feel as through the world outside the boundary of the maze has disappeared or been transmuted. Of course, you can walk the labyrinth during the day, but at night those faintly-glowing lines draw you more easily inwards.

Walk the maze slowly and deliberately, allowing yourself to sink into trance. Once you've reached the middle, sit down and close your eyes. Put your hands flat to the ground. If nothing comes to you immediately, you may choose to imagine that you are looking into a large mirror at this point. What do you see there? Something beautiful or something terrifying? A bit of both? Is it a monster that has been given life by your own fears, shame, and doubt, or do you see a glowing figure—a saint, an angel, a faery, a King or

Queen, a hero or heroine. No matter what you see it's a part of you, or could be.

If you don't have the space available to create a maze that you can walk, an alternative is to draw a maze on a piece of paper or on a flat piece of wood or stone and set it up in your ritual space. You can hold it in your hands or lay it on the floor right in front of you. Gaze at the drawing, following the twists and turns with your eyes as though you were actually walking it in some hedge garden or an ancient stone labyrinth on a mountain or hill.

With each "step" you take, feel yourself going down deeper and deeper into the Earth, down and down, until you finally reach the center. Continue to stare at the maze, letting your gaze go out of focus. If you feel inclined, close your eyes and go with any trance state that comes.

There are many maze patterns available. Some of them have come down to us from ancient times, while others stem from the maze-craze of the 16th, 17th, and 18th centuries. Some are simple, while others are marvelously complex.

(sample patterns can be seen in the illustration on page 146)

This chant can be used while you walk the maze or be spoken before taking your first step:

> **Twist and turn**
> **Spiral and flow**
> **Round and down**
> **We walk**
> **We go**
> **To thread the maze**
> **To pierce the heart**
> **Of ancient days**
> **The dreaming spark**

To be
To know
To return above
To dance the art

You can also say this first and then just use the first four stanzas as you walk the maze:

Twist and turn
Spiral and flow
Round and down
We walk
We go

Saying it in a very easy, rhyming way is best. If you can match it to your steps that's even better.

You can also dance a maze pattern, holding hands or not. One way to dance the maze without actually drawing one is to first create a large circle with an opening. Have everyone hold hands and follow a leader as he or she takes you spiraling in and around over and over until everyone is gathered in the center.

Words that can be chanted or sung while doing a dance:

Mirror mirror
Cross the maze
Turning outward
Turning in
Round about
Whirl a day
Begin begin begin again
Ee oh ee oh
Ee oh vay

Or you may use the following:

We turn
We spin
We weave
We end
Only to begin again
Follow in
Follow out
Brothers
Sisters
Shadow
Spark

Once everyone is in the middle, all can sink down and touch the earth. A sound or call may be used at this point. When each person gets a vision, they can then rise and leave, spiraling back outwards again around the group until they reach the outer edge of the circle and the entrance. They should walk away and not look back.

Spirit Familiar Rite

This ritual is to ask Ariadne to help you gain companions along your path, whether they take the form of physical people you know in this world or those who do not exist here physically at the present time. They may be called by many names, from spirit contacts or guides, even familiar spirits or familiars, but part of what they are here to do is to help with advice, insights, and to aid in any magickal or creative work that you may do.

One way of expressing intent in conjunction with this ritual is by clearing a space in your home in anticipation of their arrival. When your companions appear, in whatever form they take on, you can fill that space with items that they like or that remind you of them. It may be signs or tokens which symbolize them, or something that you see one day and that they tell you to get because they like it or are attracted to it. In many cases, when it comes to these kinds of tokens they may appear as gifts from other people or you may stumble across the perfect item at a garage sale or in a store.

For example, one day I found a broach in an antique store that had a bird with his wings outstretched and a wheel below it. I had been looking for a token for one of my spirit familiars, whose symbols included a sparrow and the ability to be all places within the circle. The moment I saw it, I knew it was the right object. In addition, I bought this spirit guide an amber and sterling silver ring, one that's far more his style and taste than mine so that when I wear it I feel even closer to him, similar to the way I feel when I wear a gold and ruby ring that once belonged to my great uncle.

The most important part of doing this rite is not the rite itself, but the emotion we extend out to call these others to us. Emotions don't just fuel the magick, but help create the connection. Ariadne tells us that *"it is not enough to ask, but we must open our hearts to those who shall come, to those who shall be our companions, our* friends, our guides, and our family—both here and across the veil, those who live in worlds both seen and unseen. Above all, we must love them, for love is the key which opens the door. Love is the path and the star which lights the way we must all walk."

Create a circle and then clear the altar of all objects.

Place a candle in the middle of the altar and light it. Light your candle from this candle. If working in a group, anyone who desires this connection should light their candle.

Hold up your candle and say:

> Ariadne
> I call upon you by your silver web
> By that which binds
> With threads of light and life
> Mad passion and delight
> Let my own light
> Shine as bright as any other
> One star
> In a trembling sea of stars
> Let me come at last to meet
> And to know those who will
> To be
> My companions along the way
> Let me see and know
> Those who have always been with me
> And always shall be
> Mine as I am theirs
> Open my heart
> I pray
> To your boundless gift of vision
> To the as yet unknown
> To all that is love
> And the art

Inborn and eternal
Brother to beauty
And sister to strength

Alternative invocation:

Dread lady of stormtide
And madness
Of lovely bliss and pain
The secret pearl
Within us all
The hidden dream of the art
By the law of the sea
I call you
By love I ask
Grant to us
Companions along the way
A bridge across worlds
Familiar as yet unknown
Unremembered
Ever was and ever meant to be
Cast us not
To the outer darkness alone
But count us among the company
Among those
We most love and adore
Bestow on us your blessings
By the shining web of light
The ever-turning wheel of time
And the constant
And beckoning polar star

Have everyone who is seeking a companion, a spirit familiar, turn towards the outside of the circle and hold up their candle. Each person may then say what comes to them to say. Your heart should be guided by what you seek. The most important part is to be emotionally open and to send out a part of yourself to guide that spirit to you, for what you send out is what comes back to you and what you get is what you need.

You may also use these words or some of them:

> **By love come to me**
> **By light I am here**
> **We who have been parted**
> **Shall part nevermore**
> **Together we shall walk**
> **As together we have always been**
> **For what makes us as one**
> **Is all**
> **The rest illusion**
> **The tides grant us this time**
> **Eternal as we live the dream**
> **And eternal reside**
> **In each other's arms**
> **Our hearts the bridge**
> **Our hopes the path**
> **That lies before us**

When all have spoken, turn and put your candle flame into the central flame. All can then dance and spin around the altar, singing a song you've chosen ahead of time or simply making a sound, a call. The whole time, you should remain open and keep focused on those others being guided to you by the light and the song.

Raise the sound to a crescendo, with your candles upraised in the middle of the circle, and then blow them out. It might be a good idea to have a feast while still in circle, sharing any impressions or feelings with each other.

Take your candle home and light it each night until it has all burned away, each time with the same intent. You may also like to set an extra place at the table when you eat, anticipating the company that will be arriving.

Ritual of Blood and Wine

Everyone should wear masks for this ritual. It's best to create your own and you can even do this as a group project ahead of time. They can be simple or complex, but they should represent a power or animal or feeling that means something to you. It could be a part of you that you want to emphasize or a power that you want to court. Meditation or divination can be done to discover what you might want to do or it might come to you in a dream. Masks can also be hung on the walls or on the stands that hold the quarter candles.

You will also need a pole and a mask and a piece of fur or fake fur that you can hang on the pole. This is if you don't intend for the God to be invoked into the Priest. Otherwise, the mask should fit the Priest and the piece of fur can go over his shoulders or be wrapped around him.

You will also need a long length of red ribbon, long enough to completely encompass the people in the circle with a little extra. Red wine and a goblet are also needed, though you can also use a small bowl.

The rest of the group may go skyclad for this rite or wear simple robes.

Cast a circle as usual. The altar should then be moved to make enough space to dance.

Light the North candle, saying:

> **To the North**
> **The darkness gathers**

Light the East candle, saying:

> **To the East**
> **The light returns**

Light the South candle, saying:

> **To the South**
> **The fire is kindled**

Light the West candle, saying:

> **To the West**
> **We hear the call**

The Priestess invokes Dionysus at this point. You can use a pinecone-tipped wand or a wand wrapped with ivy. The Priest stands to the West, his hands crossed over his chest and his head bowed.

The Priestess points the wand at the Priest, saying:

> **Lord of the play**
> **Lord of the mask**
> **By the wine of life**
> **By the drink of the dead**
> **We invoke you**
> **King and fool**
> **Master of mystery**
> **Lover of mystery's daughter**
> **From the dark come to us**
> **By the horns of the moon**
> **You are called**
> **The crown of the queen**
> **Mad with desire**

For thee
For thee

If the God is not to be invoked into the Priest, then the Priestess should stand in the middle of the group and hold the pole as she says the words calling the God. Have someone take the wand away once the invocation is complete so that she can place the mask and fur on the Priest or on the pole with the fur draped over him or it.

If the Goddess hasn't already showed up by now, everyone should then chant:

> **Ariadne**
> **He is here**
> **Ariadne**
> **Come to us**

Continue until the Goddess is there, either the sense of Her or having actually been drawn down into the Priestess. Someone should then take the red ribbon and begin to hand it around, each person wrapping it once around their wrists as it passes. Don't tie it too loosely, but not tight enough to restrict blood flow. The ends should be tied together to make a continuous circle.

The Priestess or Goddess says:

> **This is the blood**
> **The thread of life**
> **The heritage of the gods**
> **And dead alike**
> **It is woven deep**
> **So deep it can never**
> **Be removed**
> **You are a part of it**
> **It is a part of you**
> **In the heart of the labyrinth**

197

**The dance begins
Never stopping
Never ending**

**Never stop
Never end
Never fear
Never die**

Have everyone repeat:

**Never stop
Never end
Never fear
Never die**

All should then dance around the God and the Goddess, starting off slowly and building up momentum. You may be moved to shriek or cry out, and the end of the dance should conclude with a wild shriek. Everyone should sink down with their hands upraised towards the figures in the middle, sending the energy raised directly to Them.

Afterwards, the God or Goddess may be moved to speak. The ribbon is removed and handed back to the Goddess. The God should be offered the chance to bless the wine and go around to everyone so that they may drink. If the God has not been invoked into a person, the Priestess should bless the wine and take it around.

Dismiss the God by removing the mask and fur. Dismiss the Goddess with a bow and thanks.

Feasting together after this is a good idea and will help ground out any residual energy. If you are working in a large outdoor space, you can also choose to add a part to the ritual where you process around with the mask of the God in the lead and the red thread or cord binding you in a line instead of in a circle.

Invocation of Ariadne

Have the Priestess stand to the West, her hands crossed over her chest. She can be invoked with a wand or with a goblet or bowl of saltwater. It can be placed at the feet of the Priestess or offered to her after the invocation. An object with the image of a labyrinth on it can also be used or a spool of red yarn or thread.

If using a wand, point it towards the Priestess and say:

> **Stars and shine**
> **Dream and dark**
> **By the shores we stand**
> **And call your name**
> **Knowing that upon**
> **The restless waves**
> **Our words shall travel**
> **Our hearts be heard**
> **Ariadne**
> **Thee we call**
> **Thee we implore**
> **At the foot of the mountain**
> **By the mouth of the cave**
> **At the edge of the chasm**
> **The crush of the grave**
> **To be strong**
> **To be true**
> **To be yours**
> **In all the good that we do**
> **Ariadne Ariadne Ariadne**
> **Come to us**
> **Come to us**

Symbols of Ariadne

Ariadne's main symbol is the maze, a labyrinth carved or painted on a flat round stone. A bolene can also be used, a figurine or image of a bull, of grapes, and, of course, a spool or ball of thread, preferably red. The small figurine of a spider or a drawing or piece of jewelry in the shape of a web can also be used. Two candles might be set on the altar, one red and one black, perhaps surrounded by a wreath of leaves. Of course, you can take a small bull figurine and create a tiny wreath for its neck and tie ribbons to its horns.

"A sharp blade is a mercy. Since all must travel by it, it needs to be kept well-honed. He who waits beyond the gate of my blade is the mercy-giver, and He shall enfold you in His cloak, in His arms, and offer even forgetfulness. Or He will offer knowledge, each to their own. As we all act, each to our own nature. It is what we were made for. Do not ask for it to be otherwise. Some things are beyond your control. Some things are beyond even the Gods to know.

Ask of me no riddles. I do not deal in riddles. Ask me for no kindnesses. I do not award them for what must be done anyway, for what has been well promised. Do not beg of me mystery unless prepared to receive it, for I do not suffer fools and may grant what they ask simply to see what results.

But never say I am unkind nor cruel, for I only give what is asked and it is not my way to gainsay ambition. Do not blame another for your own folly. Do not whimper and try to hide your face, to cover your eyes, and proclaim I did not know, I cannot be blamed for not knowing. You knew, or you would not have asked. In daring, you take the risk. What comes is only what you have called to yourself.

Drink or don't drink. I don't care. My cup remains whether any drink from it or not.

Like the cauldron of my sister-self, like the loom, the lake, the sea, the dragon, the star, the child, the heart, all, all have drunk and in the drinking, seen. It matters not what. The heart knows, the child laughs, the star shines, the dragon weeps, the sea keeps, the lake trembles, the loom shutters, and the cauldron...the cauldron sings. One pure note. From which all shall come to pass. But then it is not really a cauldron any more than the cup is a cup.

Drink. Drink. Or don't. I won't make you. I don't care. For that is the choice you made."

Ariadne

Part Four
The Lady of the Lake

Passing to the West

White veiled she walks
Priestess among the apples
Barefoot and free
The twilight world clinging like fog
Mist rising to veil the isle
Set upon the tides of time and apart
Colored only by the sun ever setting
One final sharp gleam
And gone eternal.

She sees
She hears
She walks
She weeps.

Men still look to the west and hope
Men still look to the west and fear
As by coiled snakes
And white gold
Red flesh and green
The gift of truth her apples grant
Change all that may be changed
What will be dared
No one can answer but you.

She sees
She hears
She walks
She weeps.

For the future becomes as the past

The heart but a seed within the cup
Bud and leaf, blossom, fruit
Exist all at the same time
As the same branch coils round
Making a circle
A tree at the heart
Wherein lies the hollow tomb of kings
The beating treasure of the grail
The cup of kingly blood.

She sees
She hears
She walks
She weeps
Her eyes reveal
What the mists might well conceal
Only for a price.

One red apple in her hand
Below her only green
She still walks with serpents
The original mark of kings.

Night is descending as She walks forward on the waters, her pale skirts flowing and drifting lightly. She is silver and She is darkness, sharp and gentle, sly and kind. She wears no mask. She doesn't need to. No one can see Her clearly because She is the veil and the Veiled One, the moon and the mist and the unseen, uncanny future. The sun passes completely below the horizon as She reaches the far shore and pauses there, gazing at those who have waited for this moment.

The two men stand together and yet alone, a sorcerer and a king, one dressed all in black and grey and one in red and gold, the shadow and the light. She knows what they have come seeking and what price will have to be paid for it. A fool's journey, with

208

an eventual and inevitable sacrifice to be made for now and for the future. This is the time they were born for, a knot in the web of light, the stone cast in the deep waters, one to send ripples coursing in all directions along the wheel of destiny.

"Lady," he calls. They call together, though one remains silent.

She opens her hands and something slowly takes shape between them. Long and supple and silvery sharp, it has two edges and two fates—one to wound and one to heal, one to create and one to destroy, one to love and one to fear. It is white thorn and black. It is stone and steel. It is of the water and yet its true nature is that of dragon's fire, the hot violent blood of the earth and of the skies. It is the sword of kings and what they have come to receive.

"What do you see?" She asks, holding the blade lightly. The gold and black of the dusk glints along it, shadow and flame.

"A beginning," the king replies.

"An ending," the sorcerer responds.

"Foreshadowed and sworn," the Lady breathes. "Yours is the knot which shall be undone, releasing the dragon, turning the tide, making the golden court upon the golden hill, the place where crown and sword unite. You know this well—that the future rests upon the foundation of the past. This is the blade of the snake and of the sacred mountain. Would you take it, even knowing what is to come?"

She holds up the sword towards the sky and blue-green Witch fire spreads out from it, forming a crossroads, four and one, above and below, the link between the living and the dead.

"I shall," the king says. "And I will not forget."

209

The Lady holds out the blade towards him and the king takes it, the light fading as it touches his mortal flesh. The man in black reaches out to trace it with the tip of one finger.

"Mine is the cup," the Lady says. "But not the quest. Mine is the crown, but not the lord who wears it. Mine is the blood, willingly given in token. For I am not the Queen, but the Queen's shadow, as you...my lord Myrddin, are the shadow of the king. Are they riddles then?"

"I have no time for riddles," the king answers. "I have my responsibility."

The man who moved in the dark, who was of the dark, shook his head. "Life is a riddle," he said. "In death, the answer."

"To die is to return," the Lady said as She began to walk back across the lake. "To return is to not forget." She began to sink down into the waters, her silver dress turning to mist, to moonlight, to black weed.

They watched as the Lady disappeared back from where She had come. Only then, did the king turn towards the other man. "Will death be my answer?" he asked.

"You will never die," the other replied. "For that is not your fate. Not so long as men have faith and dare to change that which cannot be changed."

"More riddles," the king said, though his tone was fond.

"Some things, sadly, cannot be said in any other fashion," the seer answered. "But you have your sword and that shall have to be enough. As for the Lady, it is Her cup that I seek and Her love and all that may be gained there. More fool, I."

The king wrapped the sword within a fold of his cloak and, together, they walked away, across the land and into dream and myth and history and the hearts of men.

The Heart of the Lake

How love burns
Knowledge and flame
Long intertwined
Twins of power and desire
White and black
Night and day
King and Queen
Hope and dream
To give all you are
Your own cup
Held up to receive
By trembling hands
The morning star
The crown of peace
A pale kiss
And the flames
Brightest bliss

Mist rises along the shores of the lake, a dark forest gathered close around it, gently cupping and protecting the serene waters below. They are dark, deep and cold, seemingly bottomless, fed by ancient springs whose names of power have long been lost. The lake is many lakes and yet it is one, as the Lady of the Lake is one and many. If She holds a sword in one hand, the other bears a cup, both plain and glorious of aspect, shining with an inner light.

She has many names and none, for Her name is different for everyone. We know Her by Her title—the Lady, the Lady of the Lake. We call Her a priestess and so She is. We call Her a queen and so She is. We call Her a goddess and so She is. She is none of those as much as She is all of them. Meerghan, Viviane, Nimue, Fata Morgana, Morgan le Fey—no matter how lovely or mystical the name, like most Goddesses, She is as much Her title as Herself.

213

The word Lady means she who is the kneader of the loaf, as Lord means he who guards the loaf. Loaf is an old word for bread, bread which is symbolic of life and of the harvest, of the bounty of the land and the people who live there. The Lord protects life, while the Lady gives it form. From the Lord comes the fire and spirit and from the Lady the clay, the flesh made of water and of earth.

But which lake is She the Lady of? It isn't really any particular Lake that might be found in the wilds of England or France, though many can be representative of it just as certain mountains are representative of the Mountain which is the home to Gods and the gathering place of Witches of old. Sure, there are magickal bodies of water everywhere around the world, but the Lake is symbolic of the gateway. It's a means of communication and communion with the Otherworld, the land of the dead. Just as lakes and pools and wells and rivers are where power and ideas and dreams and visions emerge from the great unknown, from the elsewhere.

The Lady says: *"The mist comes, it rises. What lies within the mist are the specters of the past, the dead you have known and who know you. The ghosts of the lake, the lake which is the way, or one of them anyway. From whence do you think the power of the sword came? The dead of the land gave rise to it. They set their mark upon the King of the land, as they do upon those who keep the old blood fast and each blade they hold is the same blade. The same holds true for the cup. The King's cup or the Queen's, it matters not. Once it was the Queen's, once it was her, as the blade stood in the stead of the King. For this time and this place, however, it must be shared. It will be shared, until the stars spin it apart again."*

In the legend of King Arthur, the Lady of the Lake gave him the use of the shining sword known as Excalibur or Caliburn. This sword represents Arthur's right to kingship over England, as well as tying him to the life force of the county, making him its Lord-Protector as well as its chosen sacrifice. The two go hand-in-hand.

Out of the waters came the sword that linked the world of men to the realms of light, the realms of the Gods. When Arthur wielded the blade, he represented the power of the Divine, a power tempered by the love within the sacred cup, the cup also known as the Grail. Cups hold while swords direct, one being a male power and one a female. The Lake holds, so the sword which came from the depths of the Lake directs that bounty of energy made available by tapping into the realm of Other.

We know it well even if we don't know it—the story of Lancelot and Arthur, Morgan le Fey and Guinevere, of the blade of kings and the son of dragons, of love and chivalry and loss and rebirth. It's a part of us, the knight's quest for the Grail whose riddle will heal the wasteland, the shining castle upon the hill, a Golden Age past that will return again. We all know the tale or some permutation of it. It has been told and retold, not the least being because it's a story of passion and we are all drawn to passion.

Arthur's place and power lies in the Tor, the mountain, the hill where the earth meets the sky and where the *heiros gamos*, the sacred marriage, takes place. He is the blade to Guinevere's cup, just as the Lady of the Lake is the cup of the waters, the magickal and divine aspect of the Queen of the land. The mortal Queen, the White Queen, Guinevere represents the Lady's strength in the mortal world, while Merlin is the Black Man, the hidden one, the shadow. He is a shadow of Arthur's bright kingship.

Arthur was the visible aspect of Otherworldly power and Merlin the Unseen, the invisible power behind the mask. In much the same way, Guinevere as Arthur's Queen represented the visible aspect of the Goddess, High Priestess to Arthur's High Priest, Lady to his Lord, while the Lady of the Lake was match to Merlin. In this way, the balance is created, and a reflection. Arthur and Guinevere as Lord and Lady of this world and Merlin and the Lady of the Lake belonging to the one that lies beyond the Veil.

Arthur and Guinevere invested Camelot and the land with the living light and their love made the kingdom bountiful and great. The shadow which stands behind them, the shadow of the Gate through which this divine power came, are those shades are known as Merlin and the Lady of the Lake. Black and white pillars, each stands sentinel, while the gate between them ties together the eternal and the earthly lands. But if we are to equate the Lady of the Lake with the black pillar, and if we should decide to name her Morgan le Fay, the fay in question are not the floating and shining beings of the Air, they are not of the Seelie, but the Unseelie Court. She is Queen of the rushing horde, those who spin in the deeps, creating the currents which flow out through all worlds above and below.

Of course, there are countless permutations of Arthurian legend. The one that is most well known today is primarily based off of Sir Thomas Malory's *Le Morte D'Arthur* from the 1400's. In this version, King Arthur's parents are Uther Pendragon and Igraine and Arthur is conceived through the magickal trickery of Merlin. Arthur is raised in ignorance of who he is until he is brought to pull the sword from the stone, an act which will indicate who is right and true heir of all England.

Arthur does this, of course, but then has to fight first for his rights and then to defeat the many enemies clamoring at the borders of his country. In order to help him, Merlin takes the young King to the Lady of the Lake and She grants him the mystical sword Excalibur (*Caliburnus* in Latin and *Caledvwich* in Welsh). Arthur goes on to create a fellowship of knights who sit at the fabulous Round Table, a dowry gift of his wife and Queen, Guinevere.

Grand adventures are had by all and Arthur rules with a kind and just hand, drawing to him and his court the best of the best. It's then that a handsome and noble knight from France first appears, Lancelot du Lac. Queen Guinevere and this new knight fall madly in love with each other. This love breaks the kingdom apart. The

Quest for the Grail begins, further decimating the court, and Arthur's son, a bastard child born of his own half-sister, Morgause, rises up to overthrow him. Arthur defeats his son and rival at the last, but is mortally wounded in the process. Excalibur is finally returned to the Lady of the Lake and the King is borne away to Avalon by three Queens, there to rest until England needs him once more.

The story of King Arthur is a great myth, one of the great myths that inform the Western psyche. Some aspects of the story remain constant over time, while others change and in changing reflect the current society that gives rise to them. Is it a pagan story? Is it a Christian one? Is it about the conflict between the two? Is it a story of female empowerment? Or of a spiritual quest that defies time? Is it history or is it myth or some strange combination of the two?

No matter, Camelot casts a long shadow on the past and the future. Just as Arthur's influence extends on all that came before him, that which foreshadowed him, and all that came after. For any great event, any great time, any great king or hero or teacher, casts the shadow of their being in all directions. Their spark is so strong that it creates a knot in the web of Fate.

The castle on the hill, the gleaming golden city of Camelot, is an emblem of the crown, a crown that is also the symbol of the king and his link to Divine power and will. The Round Table within the castle is the circle, the Wheel of Fortune, where all are equal before Fate. Credited to the creation of Merlin, the Table is where a marvelous company unexpectedly appeared at the wedding feast of Arthur and Guinevere—a white hart or roebuck chased by a white hound and followed by a lady in white. Visions of the Otherworld, they represent the intersection between myth and reality, between this world and the Unseen realm. They presage the inevitable and eternal Quest.

The Lady of the Lake asks us *"who are you and who am I? My gift lies in the reflection, in what comes from the deeps. A resounding **yes**, that is what is required most of all. No matter what comes of it, embracing it all is what matters. Men fear what they do not understand. Therefore, I say understand all and you shall not fear. What you fear has power over you, far better to have such power over yourself and fear naught.*

Most of all, do not fear death, for not only have you walked its path many times before only to return to the world above, but know that death is but an illusion as much as it is a world. So that what men name death is a door, the ending illusion and the passing on inevitable. I am the Queen in the vale of apples. I know such things as I know and see you all, past, present, and future. Are you were, are, and will someday be, all one and the same within the glass, the bowl, the pool, the well, the lake.

You stretch backwards and forwards, your shadow moving with you. Harlequin. The dreaming dark. White chances and black. The greater the light, the greater the shadow. The light cast from a king is greatest of all, save for that which cast the first shadow, the shadow that we all walk."

A king exists in accord with destiny, in a conscious choice and acceptance of What Must Be. He is attuned to the flow, to the currents of power, and is able to use that current to its fullest. He writes his own fate, but he does not deny destiny. Instead, he works with destiny, a much more fruitful endeavor. For if fate may be construed as the minor arcana in a Tarot deck, then destiny can be seen as the major arcana—forces which are unalterable and meant to be, meant to happen.

Why should we fight what cannot be changed? Instead, we should fight the good fight for what can be changed, even what *must* be changed. We need to act in accord with our highest nature, our purest essence, all that a king represents. Though, of course, first we have to figure out what our true essence is before we can begin to act in accord with it. Just as in the story, when we do not act in accord with our deepest, our highest selves we are lost as Arthur and the land were lost. We wander in *Terre Gaste*, the wasteland of broken dreams and lost chances. We tremble on the edge of the void of self-destruction.

We have to pass through the shadow and find the Grail that holds the spark, the seed of light, and begin anew. Not an impossible task, but a difficult one, especially when we are far more used to doubt than surety. We often feel oddly safe in a world where others tell us what to do and what to feel because we have lost touch with our own inner selves and feelings. It's hard to stand firm and strong when we've lost our balance and our foundation somewhere along the way, especially if we don't know quite where we lost it or why.

One clue lies in the world around us. Whenever we are trampled upon, even in the name of mercy or kindness or friendship or, worst of all, in the name of love, then we stand in the wasteland. Whenever our true nature is denied or restricted, by our own hand or by the hands of others, then we stand in the wasteland. Whenever fear or doubt or anger or hatred rules us, then we stand in the wasteland, a land that desperately needs to be healed and made whole again.

There is but one way out at this point. We must go on the Quest and reclaim the cup which contains the knowledge of what was lost. Like many quests, it may start with a vision—a bright and shining image beckoning us towards the wild unknown. It may begin with a comment, a picture, a movie, a book, anything that stirs us to see that everything is not as it is meant to be and that we must do something about it. Like a light suddenly coming on in a pitch-black room, we become aware that the darkness is not all there is, though we began to think it was.

Vivianne asks us *"what is the Grail? If you do not know, then you shall not find it. To find it is to know it, and you who do not know*

219

may see it and yet not know it. Thus, to seek is to see and to see is to seek, a vision not born of the eyes but of the heart. For the door of the heart is the Grail and so the Grail is different for all. And yet there is but one Grail and therein lies mystery.

What is a riddle but a question not understood. Though some riddles the mind may not unravel, marvelous instrument though it may be. Still, it is but a tool and tools must be discarded in time if you are to proceed into the greater world. But for that you need the Grail, and so the riddle is complete."

In the old tales, the Quest was often begun by catching sight of a white stag at the edge of the forest, an image that tantalized and amazed. Or it could have started by hearing a snatch of unearthly music coming from within a fairy mound, an ancient barrow or sacred cave. Sirens called sailors to haunted islands at risk of their ships and death upon the rocks below. Spectral figures crooked a finger and beckoned for sleepers to follow. The form changes and yet the challenge remains.

Each and every quest is a quest of self for no matter how outward the journey might seem, we also spiral inwards. As the Lady says *"the lake holds all, but what emerges must first be visited in men's dreams, must be fashioned of their needs. It is not good to dream without need, for such dreams are but fancies and will not long satisfy. If you do dream, then dream well. Dream of that which the world desires and have the heart to make it true, the heart of old, a king's heart fashioned of gold, the tongue of the sun. The crown represents eternity and the scepter power, but where lies the truth if not writ upon the heart?"*

Another name for this power is simply Mystery. Others might name it Love. There is no greater magick and no greater force in the universe, though we cannot understand it in its entirety. We can only seek extraordinary vision, the kind of sheer *knowing* usually called the Second Sight or simply, the Sight. For in order to

220

comprehend Divine Mystery, we must *experience* it, not just think about it. We must learn how to look beyond the surface of things and the way to gain this ability involves the Quest.

Once we have claimed our true power, as Arthur claimed the sword that symbolized his, we can begin to change the world. As king, Arthur wielded the power of making and, with it, created a kingdom, a kingdom that reflected his own heart. Not just an earthly kingdom—if, indeed, the story of King Arthur has any basis in historical reality—but a kingdom of the spirit. A kingdom that has its existence in the Great Story, an undying story of the immortal King, the immortal kingdom, the shining city on the hill which symbolized a golden time of peace and of plenty, of justice and truth. Even the ending of the tale represents a beginning, for Arthur passed into the West, to the land of Faery and of the dead and will someday be born again from that place.

The isle of the West, Avalon, takes its name from apples, apples symbolizing wholeness and immortality. Golden apples have appeared in many old stories, a fruit so luscious and desirable that the Gods Themselves fought over it. Apples are also linked to love and, like the pig, were a gift from the realm of the dead. Which lends a deeper meaning to the Yule tradition of bearing in the head of the pig with an apple in its mouth—they are both gifts for the tables of the living, a feast laid out and provided by the dead for those beloved relatives yet alive.

Apples have an ancient association with Venus. She won the golden fruit when Paris had to choose which of the three Goddesses before him were the most beautiful—Juno, Minerva, or Venus, the glorious and powerful Queen of the Gods, the Goddess of Wisdom, or the Goddess of Beauty. They each offered Paris a gift if he would pick them and Venus was the one who won him over at the last. She offered Paris a beautiful bride in exchange for his vote. She offered Paris love instead of wisdom or power and it was love that he surrendered the apple for.

221

The city of Camelot is also equated with the color gold. Like red and purple, gold is the color of kings. Crowns are often made of gold and other precious things, stones that have various virtues and symbols associated with them. Each crown, in a way, tells a story and represents that which is most kingly and good. Just as a crown represents the shining halo of the sacred, be they a saint or king or queen, those we look to for inspiration, to see how we may live the story and each wear our own crown.

Our Golden Age derives its power from fire, from the Divine spark within each of us. We can make our own Camelot, finding our way from the wasteland and making the world bloom again. The story of Arthur is our story. The characters that live within it also live within us, archetypes of the golden kingdom of justice and compassion, the misty island of the dead, the cup and stone and throne and sword of destiny.

Myth, Story, and Legend

For past the boundaries
Of broken glass and barbed thorn,
Past must and must not
And all we were told could not be,
Past pain and fear cursed to live
To die in the tomb of hope…
A new star rises yet on the horizon.
The first star
In the highest crown of heaven
Brilliant and golden and eternal
And weeping of shadow's love
A star that no box may keep,
Nor shroud destroy

The Muse takes an active part in the unfolding story of humankind. Her heroes and heroines are larger than life because magick and mystery attaches itself to them and to their lives as each generation pins their own dreams and aspirations on them. Eventually, they may even be thought of as divine or semi-divine, what we aspire to know and to do and to be.

We do this by living our story, for each of our lives is a story. When you put all those stories, all those lives together, you create the Great Story, a mysterious tale in which we play both the part of the teller of the tales, as well as part of the tale itself. We are masters of the chessboard and pawns upon the board at the same time, moving as we must move and yet also moving as we will to move. The two work together to make the web, the tapestry that changes and changes not.

If a story in a book is inspired, if it is magickal and marvelous, then how less so can be a tale that's written into the flesh, into the fabric of the world. We hook into a channel of creative expression in

223

order to make Art and we can hook into that same channel to make of ourselves and our lives an Art, a thing assured and conscious of its Divine nature.

All things have to get their start somewhere and stories spring to life from that somewhere. But not just stories, for our very lives spring from elsewhere. We come from elsewhere as we pass through life, leaving and returning again. The line between fiction and non-fiction is thinner than might be imagined. In a way, we are all fiction. We are fictions created by the Great Storyteller. We are all masks for boundless powers, unconscious of that most of the time, so that seeking an awakening includes learning to comprehend what comes through us to the world. It's how the tapestry is woven, the web spun, the wheel turned.

Yet at the same time that we are the story and the mask, we are also the storyteller and the makers of masks. We are the Art as much as the artist. The Divine weaves the threads of Fate and we weave the threads that dance and transform, which spark and arch and pass and fade, only to be renewed. We live and we die and that creates the pattern of our thread, a pattern that changes and yet remains steadfast and true. That undying spark is who we really are, no matter what face or what form we wear. It is our Fey self, our fate. It is our Muse, the reflection made in the water of the lake, the secret hidden in the cup of the Queen.

The Lady says: *"Grant the sword to those who come to me who know my name. It is not a riddle, but the answer to a riddle, and he who does not know his own name, who has not once drunk from the cup, cannot claim the blade of promise, that which pierces the land though it was born of the waves. Just as he who has not known the cup cannot raise the castle nor command a court upon the highest hill of hills, the crown which both wears and is worn.*

I am softer than my sisters, but no less true. My dreams still have the power to bite, to pierce those who most fear their pain, to slay dragon

224

and dreamer alike. My vision has been seen reflected upon the sky as much as within the water, and though I am not heaven's queen, I am heaven's daughter. No mere priestess, but she who walks in the sleep of priestesses, showing them all they may be if they but take up the crown and veil.

I do not rule, but dream. I do not command, but coax. I do not deny, but hope. For hope is the spring eternal, and the blade was made as much of hope as of the fire. The fire upon the hill. The fire within the soul. The crown upon the king. The sword within the stone. Where blade and cup unite, there I am and yet do not remain. For mine is not the wine, but the name, the riddle of kings and knights and knaves, of the beginning and ending of days.

Do you hear a whisper? I am there..."

We are each a cup and blade of power, a sword to wield our true dreams. If we are brave and true enough, if we become kings of our own fate, we can do the impossible. It's part of the heritage of all human beings, but especially those who have awakened to the magick within them. We have the power, if we choose and realize how to choose, to create and un-create the world, to create and un-create ourselves.

What Arthur learned from the Grail was his true name and his true heart and the meaning of his life. No two people would see the same light shining from the cup for no two people are the same, nor are their fates alike. Each person has many forms, many lives, many names, yet they also bear one true name. This name represents their Divine aspect and being. This is the secret name of a Witch or cunning one, a secret that they need to protect because it's their wellspring of power and can give others influence over them if found out.

The names of the Gods and other entities have power over Them, as well. When we use one of Their many names, we are asking for a particular aspect we want to interact with. In ancient times, there was Aphrodite *of the Bow* and Aphrodite *of the Bear*, just as Hera was both a Goddess of marriage and a Goddess who protected children. Related concepts, but not quite the same. The many names of the Lady of the Lake also bears this out, for each name is a slightly different aspect. For example, the color blue has many different shades from navy to powder to robin's egg, yet all are still blue.

Queen, Lady, Priestess, and Witch...the different crowns that the Goddess wears is a mirror of the same crowns that each woman and Priestess may wear. Just as the different crowns, the different names, that the God wears is mirror to that which all men and all Priests may wear. We take on many names, many masks, during our life and even more through our lifetimes. Still, the core of us remains our own personal pole star, the purest form of our connection to the Divine fire, one sometimes symbolized by the North Star, the centermost point around which the heavens spin.

Not surprisingly, stories revolve in the sky, as well, stories of Gods and Goddesses, of heroes and of kings, of how things began. We stand below that sky and it turns above us, the stories that it tells finding their echo inside us. We are all a part of that great unfolding, and though our own stars may not be as brilliant as those of the Gods, they may eventually come to that. It remains up to us to dare to take that first step and carry on through, to stay the course and strive ever towards that star, the star of silence, wisdom, being, and essence.

The daring to strive is of the West, of emotions and of the waters. We seek the golden apples of the sun, the apples that are the fruit of the Otherworld and of the Gods. The gifts of the Muse are like the seeds of the apples and we are those same seeds. Like seeds, we spring from the ground, from the flesh of the dead, and rejoin life, rising and blossoming and leaving our gifts, our fruit, behind to keep the cycle going. Just as King Arthur is the once and future

226

king, the sewer of seeds, and the fruit that springs from those same seeds, the planter of seeds for the next year, the next cycle. Which is another way of saying that the king and the land are one, so that what happens to the king is reflected in what happens to the land.

The individual person who has taken on the role and title of king may come and go—he may die as all men must die—but his kingship remains intact, passing down to his successor, preferably one of the same royal bloodline. Like the Witchblood, when it's passed down through the blood, from one King to the next, the current of power grows stronger and stronger, evolving as the land and the people evolve. Even someday evolving a living consciousness of its very own.

Once and future and eternal, Arthur is the same lord for the same land. Just as those Witches and cunning folk who are made guardians of the land return again and again, born back to the same place and to the same blood. Renewing themselves in the well of memory and growing ever stronger. For Witches are—or should be—as much tied to the land as the king of the land, especially as they are, along with the Fey, guardians and keepers and healers of that place and the people who live there.

For this reason, we seek to see the Unseen, to have the Sight. We yearn to open the door of vision and to wake. When we wake, we become as kings, mindful of our place in the order of things and channels for the essence of who we were always meant to be. We bring something otherwise unknown and unknowable to life in the world, what is unique to us. We don't just drink from the Grail, but become as the Grail—where others then may drink of us.

The Lady of the Lake represents the wellspring of kings and of the land. She is the door through which the dream of Camelot was born; through it was Arthur's blood and sweat and sacrifice, his desire and courage and willingness to do what must be done, which brought it to fruition. As the waters give birth to the blade, the sword of fire, the godly weapon, so the Lady made Arthur the blade, the flame, a god—though it was always his right and choice to take hold of what was offered or not, to ride the blazing trail of his own star, the star that symbolized and marked his destiny.

She tells us that *"the rising of Arthur, of Arthur's star, was heralded by a sword, the blade of promise. This is the symbol which has been carried forward, which yet has the power to stir the hearts men. Each symbol fits the time and the place as much as the King. Each symbol bears both a dark and a light aspect. Each symbol may both create and destroy, for all things, especially great things, have their echo and their shadow and the shadow of some is very long indeed.*

Both the light and the shadow must be claimed by the King or King he is not. Both the past and the future find their moment in him. Both divine and mortal, he must be aware of that which he is and that which he is not. Kings are born and not made, but yet a King is made by choice and by design, by dream and by courage to carry the dream. Not just his own dream, but the dreams of all. For the two must become as one."

We have the same choice as Arthur, the same power to choose. What the sacred waters offer us may not be Excalibur, but no matter. We affect our own inner stories through the story that takes place in life and in our rituals, just as we can be influenced by stories we are drawn to in books and movies. Through them we can explore our inner strengths, our talents, and the power of our faith.

But in order for us to touch that story we have to be emotionally engaged. Intellectual thought, no matter how well honed or useful, how highly prized in today's world, cannot make all the connections. That requires emotion, the emotion of the West and of daring. It requires bringing together the Four Elements, upon which anything can be built. These elements not only create the world around us, but they create our own inner landscape, as well.

We must master them all to master ourselves; for what we built within influences what exists around us. Those that we care about and interact with, that we do magick with, share with us the ability to construct an even greater foundation together. We can call to being a great crossroads, one able to bring even mightier things into existence. One person can deeply affect another, but a group of like-minded people can change the world. Not only that, but until we learn how to step back and see ourselves and our lives and not be wrapped up so tightly in it, we can see it in those we interact with. We can use them to help us find our balance and discover our personal story.

What is the Great Story? What was Camelot really that it lingers so strongly within us?
Camelot is remembered as a time when great deeds were done, a brief and Golden Age. It doesn't really matter if Camelot ever really existed, because Camelot is an archetype. Camelot is a part of the spiritual psyche of the West. We believe in it and feel it and it becomes real to us. It doesn't have to have anything to do with history because it's part of our breath and blood and bone, our ancestral legacy.

Stories like that of King Arthur teach us about daring, about the need to take risks, and believing in and working towards what is meaningful to us no matter how hard it might become along the way. It teaches us to not give up, to not let go of our dreams, to hold fast to who we are, even in the midst of trial and tribulation. Now, the trials and dangers that a hero undertakes in a story are probably more extreme than most of us will ever know or might even wish to know, where the real heroism lies is in the *inner* battle.

As the Lady puts it: *"we each write our own story. Did you choose a miserable life? Then **un**choose it. You hold the power, for such was given to you. We cannot write your story, though we may send dreams and thoughts and guides and even trials along the way. Such is our role in your travails, not to test you, but to lend such aid as required* *for you to test yourself. We belong to you as much as you belong to us. We create each other.*

Your Gods are a mark of who you are. That you love them or fear them is a telltale sign of that which you love and fear within yourself. There are many Gods, many stories. Which shall you choose?

I would be loved. I would not be feared or hated or disavowed. Such is my story, but yet by my example, as by the example of many others both God and man, may this way be shown to others and known and taken up and so come to fruition beyond even that of a single mortal life.

What is immortality but knowing you love forever?"

Love in its purest expression is what is meant by "perfect love and perfect trust." Not necessarily the love and trust to be found in a relationship with another person—through we can aspire to that, of course—but the love and trust of knowing our perfect place. Though, this isn't the perfection meant in the sense of never making a mistake. It isn't being physically beautiful or always being right. This is the perfection of being who we are meant to be and living the life we were meant to live. This is the perfection of bringing into this world our own personal legacy.

When we find passion, when we follow it, we feed our spark and we fan its flame. It warms us to the core and gives back to us. The more alive we feel, the more alive we are capable of feeling, and the more our flame can reach out and touch others. When we are impassioned we make those around us feel more alive, more aware, more passionate. We not only show them that it can be done, but our energies actually help revitalize theirs.

Meerghan tells us: *"The water flows down from the mountains, from beneath the earth. Pure water, that which refreshes. The same water feeds the lake, as the same force feeds the well. A lake is simply a larger well, the gathering power of the spring. Sacrifices are made, must be made, to obtain that which lies at the bottom of the lake. No real treasure can obtained without due payment.*

The more intimate the payment, the more intimate the treasure. Blood gifts are best, but few choose to offer such today. In ancient day, blood and flesh were offered to the waters as bone was given to the flames. They sank beneath the waves with pleasure, knowing they would become as one with the lady of the spring, the ever-renewer. Only later were they given in fear, which is not as fitting a sacrifice.

The most important aspect was not the blood, not the flesh, but the hope which lies behind the sacrifice."

No dream can come true without that spark of faith and hope. We must, in a way, give birth to ourselves as much as to our dreams and creations. Of course, we also always have the choice to turn away from what we are meant to bring into the world. We have the power to deny our spark. We have the power to give it away. And, sometimes, we may do just that, seeing it as a way to end the struggle, to give up, to cease to fight, to hope, to be.

When Arthur was in the worst of his pain and despair, his heart and the land became a wasteland. Only when the Grail came to him did he remember and, in remembering, come back to life. This was Arthur's initiation, his second birth. Arthur saw the truth within the mirror of the Grail and that vision healed him. What did he see looking back out at him? What Arthur saw was his kingship, his belief in the ideal and in the sacrifice, and his love. What he brought was justice with compassion.

What do you want your story to be? What does the universe want your story to be? Where do free will and fate intertwine? By acting out of our being we will do what we are meant to do. By doing what we are meant to do we will be expressing our true being. Like Fate and Will, our being and doing are intimately intermingled. Our being is who we are, yet who we are can only come into the world through the medium of our actions. Our actions need to arise from the true inner source. When they arise from that place then we *are* acting in accord with the dictates of Fate.

Freedom is being free to write your own story. Look back and read it—then you will know. But where Freedom and Fate intertwine, when they work in conjunction with each other, we walk the road of destiny and our own inner light shines. When we walk with Fate that is when we become Shining Ones. The Fey are called the Shining Ones because they are projections of Fate and their name—Fey, Faery, Fata—is taken from the word for Fate. Witches and those of the cunning kind are Fey in human guise and can also touch that bright destiny and become shining nodes in the web of Fate. We are part of the web and part of the spider who spins the web. This is the threefold nature of Fate. One, Many, All, with the silent fourth aspect being that of None.

Sure, we make choices when it comes to our spiritual path, yet that same path must encompass not just what religious decisions we come to, but the whole of our existence. We must decide if our spirit is to have any say in our lives and we have to learn to listen to it. Our spiritual evolution is not a thing separate from our lives; it is an intrinsic part of all that we do or don't do, all we think or don't think, all we feel or don't feel. It is the backdrop of all we do here.

We are spirits encased in flesh and our meaning lies in how we choose to evolve as beings. The universe flows and we either flow with it or try to fight the current. Yet the current of fate, of destiny, cannot be easily altered or diverted and if we decide to go against it we run the risk of drowning. Yes, we can change our fate, but it must be a change that flows in harmony with the universe, a change that is needed. We cannot change our destiny on a whim or out of fear—that is a denial of our deeper self. As my grandmother would say, it's hiding your light under a bushel basket.

We must have faith in order to change Fate and faith comes from belief, from what we truly believe in our hearts. From trusting what our hearts are trying to tell us. Our hearts and spirits and bodies and minds must come together in union, forming a singular purpose and resolve. Then, and only then, may we alter fate for we have become one with Fate. We will become one with the spider who is a Goddess and yet...not a Goddess. Answer the question of who we are and we know the web of destiny.

A Prayer to the Lady of Lake

Sister to the dragon
Whose wings enfold the crystal pool
The black beyond
I call upon you
Hear me
Know my heart stands forfeit
Open to the all
What is offered by
The silver cup
The song of the sword of fate
Lady of the lake
You who are the moon's daughter
And the moon's reflection
Yours is the river
The eternal circle
We who stand
Within the rush of time
Stand but to know our destiny
What lies hidden
Beneath the sacred waters
The solar hill
Of sacrifice and marriage
Great queen
Let my path be written upon the stars
For all to see
Let my name reside within
The swirl of stars
Which are the dragon's scales
The heart of heroes
The hope of the heavens
The light proceeding
From the darkness
The light of gods and of kings

Immortal and undying
Let it be as mine own
As I am
Eternal as they

Rite to Ask a Vision of the Lady of the Lake

Place a piece of black cloth either on the floor in front of you or on the altar. A cup should be set in the middle of the cloth. Place three candles in a triangular pattern around the cup, one to either side and one opposite where you are—one candle to the East, one to the North, and one to the West. The cup is to the middle and you to the South.

Place a sheer or lace piece of cloth over the cup so that it hides the entire cup. The cloth should preferably be silver or white or grey. The cup you use can either be the cup you normally use for ritual or it can be one you have decided to use for scrying.

Alternatively, you can also choose to set a bowl, one with a black interior, in front of the cup and use this for scrying. It would be good if the water in the cup or bowl is spring or rain water, though you may also choose to fill it with red wine or red wine which has been salted.

Light the candle to the East and say:

Vivianne

Light the candle to the North and say:

Nimue

Light the candle to the West and say:

Meerghan

Focus on the cup or the bowl, holding your hands out over it, saying:

By the veil of time
What is named by men forgetfulness
Let me wake
Let me see
Let me remember
Grant a vision
Of what was
Of what is
Of what shall yet come to be
By the three cords
By the three roads
The three swans upon the lake
By the three sisters
Who dwell in the darkness
Weavers and spinners
And she who is keeper
Of the blade

Remove the veil from over the cup or bowl and stir the water or wine with the point of your blade or your index and middle fingers, saying:

By the black waters
Of night and sky
By the silver veil of the moon
The promise of the blood
Show me the pearl
Within the wine
The seed within the cup
That which lies upon the table
At the end
Of the mirrored hall of time
In the castle upon the hill

Gaze into the cup or the bowl and say slowly and softly, repeating if you like:

Meerghan
Vivianne
Nimue
Lady
Grant to me true sight

Look into the depths, into the darkness, into the blood of history. You may choose to repeat softly again and again, as a sort of mantra, either the names of the Lady of the Lake or simply the words:

Grant to me true sight

Or simple:

True sight

To look into the cup is to look into yourself as much as elsewhere. The rite of scrying is as much a way to awaken what already lies within as it is to look without. For the past and the future are one, just as the snake biting its own tail encircles all knowledge and the knowledge of all.

When you are done, recover the bowl or the cup with the veil and thank the Goddess for any visions or insights that have come. Libate the water or the wine outside.

Blessing Rite of the Lady

Cast a circle as usual.

A Priestess stands in the North with her arms crossed over her chest, her head bowed. The Priestess can have a blue or a blue and silver veil draped over her.

A Priest invokes the Lady of the Lake into the Priestess, holding up the cup filled with red wine before her.

He gives the cup to the Lady after She appears, kneeling before Her. He may then ask for himself or for the whole group, saying:

> **Lady of tomorrow**
> **Of red flesh and of white**
> **I (we) summon tomorrow**
> **By the portents of the past**
> **By the golden light of promise**
> **Five seeds entwined**
> **To charm the coming dawn**
> **The crown of kingship**
> **The mantle which encircles the land**
> **Fertile and lovely and gracious**
> **As any known**
> **By the gods or man**
> **Grant to me (us) thus**
> **The perfect unwinding**
> **Of fate**
> **Destiny's brightest blessings**
> **Upon all I (we) would create**
> **From my (our) birth**
> **Unto my (our) death**
> **A vision true and proud and free**
> **To walk**

With those ever-knowing
With the daring ones
Of old

The Goddess may speak as She is moved, before coming around to offer a drink from the cup to all in the circle and sharing any words with them.

The last of the wine should be given as an offering to the ancestors, those who came and who dared before.

If you choose to do this ritual outside of a circle, it can take place around a table shared by the entire group. A holiday-like feast can be set in waiting, with one place remaining empty for the Unseen ones. This plate and cup and the food and drink given should then be left outside if you are able, or libated beneath a tree, preferably an oak tree.

When next an opportunity comes to dare something, to take a risk, remember that this is the road you asked for, the path that is being offered. It may be something literal, such as a change of job or fortune, or it might be something where you have the choice of reacting differently than you normally might.

Grail Rite

The cup has also been known as the *Sangreal* or the Grail, *sang* meaning blood. It's the cup of the "King of Kings" or the Blood of Kings, that which makes them King, much as Arthur was called the *Ard Ri*, or "High King" for his blood was kingship itself, the very idea of kings. It's also the cup of the Goddess, of the Queen, She who gives birth to Kings and passes down the royal bloodline. The Grail is both a fruitful gift and dutiful sacrifice, an intimate link to the *sang* or blood of the mighty.

For this ritual, you may want to set a mirror on the center of the altar and light extra candles. If you have a floor length mirror on a stand instead, you can place it to the North so that the candle there is reflected in it.

A royal looking altar cloth can be used, gold and blue with the images of dragons, or purple and gold with solar or crown symbols. If you have a crown—even a plastic or paper one—you can set it on the center of the altar. Otherwise, you can use a crown woven of wheat or leaves. Place the cup in the center of the crown or wreath. The cup may be a fancy or a plain one, but it might be a good idea to pick a cup that doesn't belong to anyone in particular. You should also have a bottle of red wine ready.

Cast a circle as usual. Have everyone stand, gazing at the center of the circle.

The Priest or chosen person says:

> **We gather close**
> **Standing**
> **As a crown upon the mountaintop**
> **As a spring within the valley**
> **As the sun upon the hill**

As the moon upon the waves
We gather close
We know each other's names
As we would know yours
Lady
Keeper of the dream
We gather close
We hear your voice
Hear ours
Hear ours

Take the crown and place it on a chosen male or the Priest. Invoke
with the wand, saying:

Lord of light
King of kings
The north of being
We call you
You who have dared
The throne of peril
Willing to the sacrifice
Out of love we call you
We whose hearts
Sing with your own
We ask you
Speak to us
Share with us the voice
Of the land
Of the blood
The dragon's fire
Born of the serpent
Who encircles all

The God pours red wine into the waiting cup and blesses it. A
chosen person or the Priestess then asks of Him:

What is the need
Great one
What is required of us
We who are
Servants of the land

Listen to what the God has to say, either to the group as a whole or to individuals. Afterwards, give the God your thanks, bowing before Him. Dismiss the God by removing the crown or wreath and replacing it on the altar.

Have a chosen woman, or the Priestess, pick up the cup and hold it out in the center of the circle, saying:

This cup is all cups
The cup of life
The cup of time
The cup of death
The cup of eternity
To drink is to taste life
It is to taste death
To know yourself
And to see beyond the veil
The world of gods and spirits

She brings the cup close again and gazes down into it, saying or whispering:

This is the lake
This is the heart
This is the song
This is the soul
Of what we drink we become

Or:

Of what I drink I become

She hands the cup to her left to be passed from person to person, each taking time to gaze into the depths for any insight or message.

Before each person drinks they can repeat:

Of what I drink I become

When all have drunk from the cup, it's returned to the Priestess. She takes her own drink and libates what remains in the goblet. She returns the cup to the center of the altar and faces each person one at a time, asking the question:

And what will you become

Each person may answer or not as they choose. They may also answer silently.

Afterwards, everyone takes hands and says:

> **We are the circle**
> **We are the light**
> **We make the circle**
> **We make the light**
> **From the darkness we shall come**
> **And to the darkness go**
> **Lighting the way**
> **For those who come after**

Dance then, a slow and measured dance. The dance can be done in silence or with a pre-chosen song or chant. At the end of the dance, everyone should turn outward and envision themselves as lit candles, as beacons in the dark. A great sound should be raised at this point, either all at once or slowly building up from one voice until all have joined in. It doesn't matter if there are no words.

Bridge Between Worlds Ritual

Two goblets should be set out, preferably exactly the same. If not, then one should be silver and one gold, or one black and one white. Set a plate between them, a plate filled with small yellow or gold round cakes. It's better still if someone has made the cakes rather than bought them.

One silver and one gold candle should be on the altar, both unlit. Or the same colored candles can placed in a silver-toned candleholder and a gold-toned candleholder.

Cast a circle as usual.

The Priest or Priestess or a chosen person says:

> **Two dragons locked in battle**
> **One red and one pale**

Have someone pour red wine into one goblet and milk into the other and continue with:

> **The blood of this world**
> **And of the other**
> **Not enemies**
> **But lovers**
> **Sisters**
> **Brothers**
> **Drawn together**
> **Only to part once more**
> **Though the power of love**
> **Shall ever prevail**
> **The bridge between worlds**
> **Nothing can keep us apart**
> **Not so long**

As we remember

The red wine and the milk should be shared with all and the last of it poured into a waiting libation bowl.

The silver candle is lit by the Priest and the gold candle by the Priestess.

The Priest says:

I call upon the moon

The Priestess says:

I call upon the sun

The Priest says:

I call upon the cup

The Priestess says:

I call upon the blade

Everyone in the circle then takes turns saying the same lines, passing them around and around the circle. It can also be reduced to just:

The moon
The sun
The cup
The blade

Or even:

Moon
Sun

Cup
Blade

This should continue faster and faster, raising energy. At the final point, all clasp hands and pour the energy into the feast set before them.

The Priest and Priestess of all there may each take part in saying:

>Arthur Pendragon
>Morgan le Fay
>Lord of the mountain
>Lady of the lake
>Bless this feast in your name
>And in the names of all
>That you remain
>Artos
>Nimue
>Let us eat and drink
>Of the nature of all that is
>Eternal and free
>Beautiful and strong
>The grail of self
>And the kingdom of heaven's promise
>The compass of the heart
>And the crown upon the hill
>Where two meet
>And are made as one

Pour more red wine or milk into everyone's own goblets and raise them together in a toast, saying:

>King and Queen
>Man and woman
>Night and day
>Life and death

Here on the shores
Of the unknown dream
Our life and our legend
Begin at the last

All drink, libating the last if desired. Everyone should sit and share the cakes then, also giving one of them in libation.

Everyone should get a chance to talk about their life's story. This can be prepared ahead of time, each person trying to write it as though from the perspective of someone else looking back at their life, seeing all the forces that have moved through it, what made you what you are, and all those you have affected.

Continue on into your future, seeing it as building upon the foundation of your past—relating what will you do as though it was already done, as if your future accomplishments were already reality. Try to see your life as a whole, not a series of events but a poem, a painting, a play, a piece of Art.

The Rite of Return

Do not draw a circle. Instead, have everyone move deosil round and round at a very slow and measured pace. Everyone can take a line to say, either moving around the circle or across it as you dance. Repeat as you move, starting off slowly and then gaining speed, dancing and saying the words faster and faster until the energy peaks.

I am the flame
I am the blade
Beneath the lake
Upon the hill
The golden crown
Of the sleeping lord
I am the light
The coming dawn

I am the castle
I am the tor
The hall of the cup
The dreaming stone
I am the path
The serpent's walk
I am the dark
The waiting spark

Begin to light the Quarter candles, moving slowly as these words are said:

North:

The light and the dark

East:

Never one without the other

South:

Two hearts beating true

West:

Half of a circle and more

Finish again in the North:

Half of each other

Light a candle on the altar to represent the God and one to represent the Goddess, saying:

God and Goddess
King and Queen
Priest and Priestess

Have everyone take some red wine for their own cup or goblet. Each person should then dip two of their fingers—the index and the middle finger together—into the wine and mark their foreheads with the crossroads. They may also touch the wine to their lips thereafter, saying or having someone say:

As one we renew
The charge of old
With a kiss
With the blood
That falls within the cup
The same blood
Which marked the chosen
And those who chose

Pour some of the wine into another bowl or cup or goblet and set it on the altar between the God candle and the Goddess candle. Have everyone drink some wine from their cups, saying:

> **One for me**
> **One for thee**
> **And one for that which brings**
> **Land and king**
> **Earth and sky**
> **Mortal and divine**

Have everyone raise their blades in a salute towards the center of the circle, above the altar, saying:

> **We shall make again**
> **The shining court**
> **Upon the shining hill**
> **Descend to claim**
> **The treasure beneath the lake**
> **To wake**
> **Those who must be awakened**
> **Who sleep**
> **Among the seven standing stones**
> **The watchers from the stars**
> **By whose regard**
> **The flame within never dies**

Everyone should kiss their blades, then set them on the altar, the points facing inwards at the cup of wine that lies between the two candles. All kneel or sit around the altar and take each other's hands. Begin with a single voice, then add one after another until all are singing, one sound, no words necessary. This should continue, the sound and the attendant energy rising naturally until it reaches a crescendo.

All should keep the intent within their hearts as they make the sound, the idea of waking up what needs to be awakened and calling the powers to them. If you like, you can imagine that as you sing the light that is within you gets brighter and brighter, shining out in a great darkness, a beacon lit on a sacred hill, the hill of Kings and Gods.

Afterwards, all may sit around the altar and wait to see if any insights or visions come to them, even if you may hear voices or feel a spirit close enough to desire to speak through one of you. Use whatever technique you usually do in order to invoke this spirit into the person and to dismiss the spirit after it has spoken.

If you do not have a invocation that you have practice in using, you may simply hold the wand out before the person and have them cross their hands over their chest and bow their heads. The invoking person can then simply say:

> **Speak to us if you will**
> **We await you**
> **Good spirit and true**
> **You whom we have called**

If you do not have a dismissal that you use normally, you can simply use the words:

> **Depart depart depart**
> **To the realms beyond**

The person can then lay their hands on the earth or floor and ground out the energies. Or someone can put their arms around them, someone that the other person trusts, and have them be an anchor to guide them back.

Invocation of the Lady of the Lake

This can be used to call the Lady into the ritual or into the Priestess so that She can speak. Have the Priestess stand with a veil over her head or hair, preferably blue or silver or both. If you have a blade or sword available, place it at her feet along with a cup. Otherwise, just a cup will do.

The Priest or chosen person invokes, saying:

> By all that is
> And all that seems
> The world of desire
> And the realm of dreams
> By the wandering path
> And the good straight blade
> The flashing crown
> And the cup of kings
> Thee we invoke
> Oh Lady of the waters
> We call you
> By the light which shines
> Upon the hill of days
> The breathless shimmer
> The treasure beneath the hill
> Men's secretmost souls
> All they hold dear
> Lady of the lake
> Come to us
> Lend us your aid

Symbols of the Lady of the Lake

For the Lady of the Lake, Her main emblem is a cup. A sword may also be used, as well as a crown, the image of a lake or a castle, most especially a castle set upon a great hill, blue and silver candles, apples that are either real or artificial and honey. A clear glass bowl or goblet that you can fill with spring water or wine, preferably a honey-based or flower flavored wine.

"Shallow, shallow, shallow…we skim the surface and fear the depths. Talk, talk, talk, is that all you do? This is not the end, but the way to begin.

Use the tools and not be deceived into thinking they are who you are and what you aim to do. The tools are but tools, good or bad, meant to open the way. Do not cling to them, but use them. If they do not work, abandon them. Pass them to others for whom they may work if you must, but find the way. This is the most important part—find the way.

Better if you go by the full moon, but if not walk the dark. Both may take you there if you dare. If you walk. If you do not fear and do not fail.

All must find their own way, so do not fix yourself to another. All have that which they may teach, but find your own truths hidden in the truth of others. Do not take their truth for your own, lest it fail you when it is most needed.

You need not walk alone, yet in the end it is what we all must come to. To find we walk alone, yet never alone, and so to be a multitude and one both at the same time. The very secret of the Gods and of time and existence, a secret that cannot be known until and unless you come to knowledge of who you are and so of your own secrets.

The well of knowledge lies inside us all. Sink deep. Dream. Call out and do not fear what shall answer that call. If words will not serve you, speak not, but listen. Answer with the voice of your heart, your truest desire, the song of your blood, and the dream of your thoughts."

Meerghan, the Lady of the Lake

Conclusion

Lamia

Poets and singers, dancers all
Through their arts a dream would call
Passion and fury into being
The sharp-eyed one, the lady pale
Seeking the secrets and the power
Kept tangled in her lover's hair.

Where the White Lady takes her rest
Horsetail and feathers line her nest
All a lifetime in her smile
All of beauty in her breast
While laugh the polished bones below
Bound for a year, bound for a day
With glorious coils which cost them dear
They loved the one who loved them best.

Form of a horse and shape of owl
Serpent whose poison sweetly flows
Surrender all to seek her face
And in the burning will create
Terrible joy in her embrace
Queen of heaven, the Queen of hell.

Where the White Lady takes her rest
Horsetail and feathers line her nest
All a lifetime in her smile
All of beauty in her breast
While laugh the polished bones below
Bound for a year, bound for a day
With glorious coils which cost them dear
They loved the one who loved them best.

Nine sisters she danced in the past
Feel her touch, she comes for you
Will you run or will you dare
To seize the ring she offers true
And to her wild heart be bound
To marry the night, to ride the mare.

Where the White Lady takes her rest
Horsetail and feathers line her nest
All a lifetime in her smile
All of beauty in her breast
While laugh the polished bones below
Bound for a year, bound for a day
With glorious coils which cost them dear
They loved the one who loved them best.

Waves wash up and leave behind trinkets, but to find the greater treasures you simply have to get your feet wet. You need to brave the currents and risk the depths. Risk and reward go hand-in-hand, especially in the realm of the Muse, She who is both the ruthless monster and irresistible Siren of the Sea. We owe Her much for She gives us much, no matter how we see Her as once upon a time, in the now, or in the far-flung and undoubtedly odd future.

She has always been with us and we can see Her influence in our modern words, words such as *music, museum, amuse, amusement, bemused.* Amusements have come to mean mere entertainment, things to trifle away our time with. But amusements can be far more than that, for they are focuses for thoughts, hopes, and dreams. We are fascinated by them and pour energy and creativity into them. We can become lost in them, *bemused* if you will. To be amused or bemused can be likened to finding yourself bespelled and, certainly, we can easily find ourselves adrift in music or tranced out in contemplation of art and artifacts in museums. All offer a doorway to experiencing, seeing, feeling, and knowing differently.

We are attracted to our amusements. Not in the sense of something fun and frivolous—which has what the word has come to mean for the main part—but something that entrances us and makes the world sparkle. It serves not just as a distraction from boredom or our worries, but to make us feel well and truly alive. For real amusements are meant to touch our emotions and inspire us to acts of creation for we fix our attentions on hobbies, on movies and books and games, and that fixing of attention is power. All that focused attention creates *something*. Sometimes, it even succeeds in bringing that something to life, even if only in the shadowy world of the unconsciousness or the group soul we all share.

For what we fix our will and our imaginations to can become *real*. What we take as harmless (more or less) amusements can gain a hold on us and a foothold in our world, especially when a lot of people fix their attentions and energy on it. This is why it's important to find what impassions us and use that fixation to create what is beautiful, useful, and needful. To make an amusement that serves not just as an escape from reality, but a way to more full enter into and participate in reality. Through the Arts, through hooking into that ancient current, we can see deeper into the universe around us, understanding more than what is obvious merely through the curtain of our five senses. We can learn to see the greater world that we are normally oblivious to.

To muse on something is to focus on it, not just our minds, but our emotional intensity. This kind of bemusement wraps us up in a sort of trance, almost as though we had stepped into another world—or into a complete and utterly joyful rapport with the world we already live in—entering an altered and expanded state of awareness. It's as though we've become wrapped up in a charm of fascination, losing touch with most everything else, at least for a little while. This sort of concentration can be learned, of course, but it can also come from following and seeking that which we love. For what we love has the greatest power over us, a power that we freely follow.

263

This is the same sort of concentration that we discover when we immerse ourselves into the Arts, whichever aspect appeals the most. The trance of the Muse encompasses us and it's as though we've plunged into some great rushing current, one so real, so beautiful and so terrible, that it can even hurt. From that place, we can work marvels and bring to life something as yet unknown and undreamt of. It just flows into and through and out of us, not just a current of power, but an awareness of power.

This is the mystical world that the Arts seek to reveal to us, the hidden connections and unseen forces that really move and shake the universe. Through the Arts, including the magickal Arts, we become aware to what is going on around us, and through that awareness gain an expanded vision, the better to take an active part and conscious role in the future. With the sight, with understanding of mind, body, and blood, we can begin to play the game rather than simply being a piece on the chessboard.

As the Muse Herself says—She only gives us the truth. It's up to us to find a way to allow that truth to manifest in the world we live in. It's up to us to give that truth a name and a shape so it can project itself into the physical plane. A challenging proposition, sometimes, since many of these truths don't fit easily into the world, especially since today's version of reality tends to be restricted by a linear idea of time and a "proof" based ideology of reason.

Not that science and reason are inherently bad, not at all. It's just that they are generally limited to rather narrow view, often taking the form of an either-or rationale that doesn't work very well when you get past the surface of things. Science and reason aren't all that there is, for there are many other ways of seeing and understanding the workings of the universe and many of those older ways are, thankfully, still retained in native cultures today. We can learn from them what it is that we of the West have lost, though how we connect to those understandings must be built upon the foundation of our own past.

One of those truths is that the physical plane is but one of many aspects of reality, a reflection, an echo, a mask of the much larger and stranger reality which lies behind it. The people of the ancient world understood this far better than we do today. Yet the old knowledge still lingers and can be found if we know what we are looking for. To open up to the Muse is one doorway used by the ancients. For the Old Ones knew and answered to and pledged themselves to Her gift. They were willing to dare to pay the price.

Still, the mysteries of the Muse can only really be understood by direct experience and through emotion, by passing beyond the written word or the action into direct and immediate understanding. Dreams are, at their heart, more real than what is usually thought of as real today. Dreams flow as water flows, acting much like any other conductive force. They go deep into the earth, down into the dark, only to re-emerge to the light, carrying with them the secrets of the deeps. For where water and earth unite, there lies the cave of the beginnings, the place that existed long before time began. As the light goes down into the dark, so the light is born from the dark.

Accordingly, we need to summon up Ariadne, praise Aphrodite, call out to Cerridwen, and walk the path laid out by the Lady of the Lake. We need to court the Muse and recall the glory of Her countenance. We must rejoice in Her beauty and Her gifts. Gifts of art and magick, of feeling and daring that will lead us to mystic understanding, to healing, and to artistic expression that can bring worlds into a dynamic conjunction. Gifts that can serve and reveal the mysterious workings of the All.

We must also acknowledge the debt owed, for in the Age of Aquarius the power of the Muse will no longer be free. It will require a willingness to serve and to take part in reciprocity in order to balance out the imbalance that is our present situation. Only then can we begin to return to a much needed alignment with the workings of the nature and its cycles of "you give so that I may give,

I give so that you may give". We must recall that we are all in this together, intrinsic and interlocking parts of the great mystery

The Earth Mother and the Mother of Waters—She who is the Muse—represent two of the physical components that make up the world. Yet, they are the two components which we have the least amount of influence over; for the eternities of Earth and Water lie more in the hands of the Gods than in our hands. Fire and Air remain ours to mold, the spark and the spirit granted for each of us to bring into realization in our own way.

We need all four elements, of course. We need Earth, Air, Fire, and Water in order to exist. Earth and Water to make our physical forms and Air and Fire to bring it to life and consciousness. Life was born of the Earth, in the arms of the Earth Mother—call Her Terra Mater, Gaia, or Maman Ertah—when the fire came down from the sky. Water became blood, so the power of Water, of the West, can't help but exist inside all of us. It lives inside our blood and when the blood wakes to what it is, then it has come to know the heritage of the heavens.

We are born again and again to Being from the ashes of our own destruction in much the same manner as the Phoenix. For the Phoenix is the ancient serpent-bird, ever returning to brave and to endure the fires of transformation and regeneration, the same powers to be found in Cerridwen's cauldron. This winged serpent is Fire, the flame of the stars, the outward sign of the Mystery from which we all stem. It is love and joy without limit, boundless and free, sublime ecstasy uncoiling to fill up the physical world with light, life, and power, what can also be called the *kundalini*.

A key part of transformation lies in daring. To risk is an intrinsic part of the West, part of the acceptance of the Muse's gift. To risk our lives, our dreams, our hopes, all in the attempt to make something more, something better, something beautiful, something real. To see our best and brightest dreams come to fruition. To have some part of our lives continue on in what we have had a hand in creating, sending it out into the world unknowing of what will arise from it, whether it will be accepted wholeheartedly or trampled on.

It's the Goddess of the West that we appeal to when we toss a copper penny into a Wishing Well, when we tie a red or golden ribbon to the branch of a weeping willow tree near some cool spring, when we ask for the as yet unknown future to spin for us a world. More than a dream and less than a vision, it's to that narrow edge of possibility that we aspire, to dare to change things, to bring into being what is not just needed, but bright and beautiful. It's for this reason, among others, that we were given the right of choice.

So what do we do with that ability to choose? Well, if one is a Witch, one of the cunning folk, we decide to change things, to create and to destroy, to end and to begin, to heal and to curse, to weave stories and reality. We pledge ourselves in service to the Muse and to Her gifts, knowing that is something never done lightly, but taking that path willingly enough because, among other things, it must be walked.

But never think that the road the Muse offers is an easy one. Bright moments must be paid for in the coin of the dark for the greater the dark, the greater the light. Pain and suffering and hardship may not be comfortable and, understandably, we tend to try to avoid it, yet to learn and to grow and to evolve as a person and as an artist such pain is sometimes required. Of course, it doesn't really make the hardship any easier to face—at least, when we're smack in the middle of it—but it will make us stronger and the Arts that we produce all the more incredible.

But then we join with the Muse for this wild ride, to take the tangled and unknown path, the thin boundary between Divine touch and insanity. Worship of the Muse is the Mardi Gras of the soul, a creative release akin to the combined creation and destruction that accompanies the best sexual cataclysm. And not just the moment of absolute orgasm, but the whole hyper-aware, dream-suffused state of "being in love" finds its beginnings in Her aspect and in Her guise.

The Muse is the requisite and exquisite aspect of all that finds expression through the Arts. She is pain that is sharp and joyful and the joy that is sharp and full of pain; double-edged, just as all real gifts must be for though the gifts give much, they also require much. Not the least of which, they demand recognition, response and change at a deep level that cannot be denied. For each person that is touched by that treasure dredged up from the depths, by the painful pleasure of the Arts, spreads that power even further. As one drop becomes a trickle and the trickle turns into a stream, the stream giving rise to a river and even, on occasion, the inevitable, unstoppable flood.

An artist is a window, a channel, a gateway. The work of the artist can also *become* a gateway, a path for others to follow, not to do exactly what the other has done so much to realize that they can follow their own path. It's not really correct to say that an artist has an obligation to create, but an artist can't *not* create. We can't help ourselves. It's a burning need within us, an overpowering desire, a frantic itch, a hunger that little else can satisfy for long. This means that, though the creative process can be fulfilling, we always risk becoming addicted to that rush. Many artists have fallen from grace in pursuit of greatness.

We are mortal, locked into time, and all that we create is also mortal. Yet the feeling, the power, the idea that is expressed through our Art is not bound to time nor doomed to die. Once it has been brought into this world it takes on a life of its own, one that cannot be easily destroyed. It takes root here and though it can go to sleep and slumber for a time, sometimes even for centuries, fresh shoots, branches, leaves, buds, and the eventual fruit can still spring forth again.

268

Each blossoming builds upon a previous one. Branches intertwine, forming patterns. We live in the forest of all that has come before. We are the inheritors of countless seasons of creation, of all that has grown from the precious "seeds" stolen or given from the Otherworld, the fire of the Gods. These seeds come to rest in the earth of physical being where they will eventually germinate and grow. Even if the physical form withers, yet the idea exists and may be resurrected.

An idea comes to birth in the physical world, rises to its height, only to decline and be buried in the earth, the collective unconsciousness. There, it cannot be lost, only forgotten, save for those who dare the darkness in search of such things. For though many dreams are born, some to sleep at the last, their energies spent for a time; yet they are not truly gone. These slumbering ideas and powers make for a fertile ground, one that those on spiritual journeys can attempt to tap into.

To change the world one must work with these sleeping powers, these unseen shadows, and awaken them. When a certain critical mass is reached, great change occurs, overpowering any resistance to change. This can happen slowly or quickly, gently or violently, but it will happen. It has happened many times before and it will happen again. It's happening all the time.

There are patterns in the dark, patterns that project into the light, and these patterns effect us all. Those who work magick tap into the stored knowledge and power inherent in these patterns, the same ones reflected in the night sky. When we learn these patterns we come to an understanding of that which changes and that which does not, of the sweep of the storm, the turn of the tide, the patterns of the web and of the game. What is transformed in the dark is eventually reflected in the world we all know.

This sort of change can also happen within the inner landscape of a person, eventually transforming their outer world. It can happen for cities, countries, and our planet as a whole. The essential process is similar because it's the same pattern over and over again, smaller cogs and gears moving progressively larger ones. The Arts give expression to these patterns, both new and old. The two intertwine as the cycles weave together, creating the threads of existence.

We are dreamers, but more than that, we are doers. For, without that, what we dream can't come into its own. All that we can do may be an Art. All that we do can reach out and touch those who need. All that we may do can bring about change for we are all agents of change, of chaos and of order. The honest truth lies somewhere in the middle between the two, between what is created by the interplay of order and chaos. As it lies in what is destroyed by the two. It was the dreams and the dreamers of the Piscean Age which turned that force into the conflict of duality, just as it will be those who dream and give birth to the living paradigm of the Aquarian Age that will help shape what the next cycle of the Ages will hold.

We have to know what we shall pour that power into once we have tapped into it. We have to know what we seek to leave behind us, our gift to the world. Because all of us have the power of choice we can choose to bring joy into the world or pain, to create ecstasy or terror. Inspiration as a force is inherently neither positive nor negative, and can and has been used to either end. We are the way that this power enters our world. Our skill and our talent opens the door, but our choice provides the focus.

Emotion feeds spellwork and other forms of the Arts. Emotions are intimately tied to memory and memories are of experiences. We are the result of all that we have known and done and seen and felt and believed—how can that which we create be any different? We create and our creations also can create—we have poured that power into them much as the Divine poured it into us. Do our inspirations inspire others to seek their own inspiration, to court the Muse? Do they serve to build a thing of lasting wonder, something that adds more beauty to our world? Or do they feed and serve ignorance, intolerance, shame, hatred, violence, cruelty and other unhappy creations? Do we ride the power or does it ride us?

The Muse is dangerous, not just because Her power is thrilling and sometimes even too much to handle, but because She brings change. She inspires change. She lets us remember that we are powerful creatures and that nothing stays the same forever. She gives us the tools to realize that we have the ability to make choices and seek our own answers, our own way; that we may not only be inspired, but inspire.

The writer, Mark Twain, once mentored a group of young women who wished to be writers and artists. He corresponded with them and gave each the gift of a fish pin, nicknaming them his aquarium. He took a keen interest in their artistic endeavors and though, no doubt, there was a bit of his well-known love of the ladies involved in all this, he clearly wanted to see them pursue and realize their own dreams. Certainly, to have the support of such a famous writer and well-known figure would have been profoundly inspirational.

Of course when we swim in the depths, there is the risk to consider, the danger of losing our way and never finding home again. This risk is not just for the artist, but for their friends, family, and community. It's a price to be paid for the future and for the world, one that has been paid many times in the past and will be paid again and again. We go into the heart of the Abyss and return if we can…shining and stronger for the journey and with some small precious gem that will have a profound effect on all that it touches.

We look around us; we look inside us, and bring out something in response. Both we and those we know are changed by it, as to experience something is to be changed by it. The Arts of the Muse are experiences channeled by a few and experienced by the many. They are meant to make us feel. We become alive through the Arts and, in the end, our life is as much an Art as any mere painting or poem. We all play our part in that story, our choices spun into the web of Fate. The same choices are reflected in the dance of the labyrinth and the deep mirrored pools of water that are gateways to all the places we could ever imagine.

Who is the Muse?

She walks in the bright meadows of morning, her touch spreading white seeds and dew. She walks in the great haunted woods, narrow shards of sunlight coming down between the trees to connect the world above to the world below. She walks upon the mountaintop, white snow swirling as a veil between the sky and the earth. She walks within the depths of the maze, a torch held in one hand and a crown of laurels in the other. She walks upon the distant most shores, barefoot and free, sure of step and light of fancy.

She is drifting beauty and the tides of gladness. She is spilt blood and sacrifice, words that can wound and words that can heal. What is history to her but the passage of Her grace, a momentary lightning glow and gone, the rise and inevitable fall of cities, kings, dreams, and all life everywhere. But then death to Her is not an ending, but the very framework for life, that which holds the mosaic together.

She is in the song, the story, the splash of color upon canvas, the ripple of notes that laughs or weeps, the graceful twirl of a hand or skirt or feet upon the earth…but most of all She is that which is in each of us; that which can be our Art, our song, our story, our passion. All it takes is acknowledgement, our desire to open to Her touch, and our willing sacrifice upon the wheel of creation.

The Muse is emotion, water, daring, but most of all She is inspiration. She wears many faces, for we each have our fears and our desires. In this way, we make Her as much as She makes us. She will be what we ask of Her to be, even if it's a frightening thing. For She is beautiful and She is terrible, more than we can stand and all that we might ever seek. To find Her within is to find Her without. To find Her without is to find Her within. She is inside the Art, inside the artist, and inside those who find themselves moved by the Art, a continuing, unwinding circle

Aphrodite, Cerridwen, Ariadne, the Lady of the Lake…these are but a scant few of Her names. She is as many and varied as any other Goddess. She is both the enchanting shimmer of light upon the waves and the cold and inexorable currents in the blackest deeps of the sea. All we have wrought, all that we have created, we could not have created without Her. For everything begins elsewhere, in the idea, the sudden flash of insight, the rippling stream of inspiration, frightening and heady. Nothing physical is begun without having begun before, without first finding a reflecting in the Other.

Power flows continuously between the land, the Gods, and the people of the land. Witches and cunning folk help to keep that flow going, ensuring that it is hale and healthy and in vital accord. If that energy is a glowing life force, then the Muse is the way it shimmers as it catches the light just so. It's the rainbow incandescence, that which makes life *lovely*. It's giving that extra bit, pushing the envelop, not playing it safe, wishing upon a star. It's putting rich butter cream icing on a perfectly good cake and making it all the sweeter. It's the agony and the ecstasy and sheer, unbridled *feeling*.

We laugh, we weep, we sing, we dance, we reach out to each other in a million ways, our emotions forging the bridge between us and our separate worlds. We must each seek our own Muse and allow that sparkle to grow, to show itself through our works, our words, all we say and do and dream and dare. Don't wait, don't even think you have nothing to offer; we all do, because that's one reason why we're here. None of came here without meaning to and each of us have something great inside us, something fresh and beautiful and crazy-in-a-good-way that we need to bring to fruition. It may take a lifetime, but it's what will make us happy when nothing else will. For those who do not dare, do not live.

Who is the Muse?

She is as much a part of the story as She is a co-conspirator with us in its creation. She breathes with us and we with Her and so we are the pens that Fate writes with and the Muse, the liquid flow of ink upon the page.

"Once, years past now, I told you who I am. Some doubted and some doubt still. Some insisted that they and they alone were the creators of their own fortunes and that they need not answer to anyone for the source of that inspiration. They are wrong.

Inspiration is no gift, but a bargain. I give. You give. I have given, but you have not, not for many years, not fully, not as you should. I have been kind. For the sake of old promises, I have been more kind than is in my nature to be. I can wait. I have waited. I have held my hand, even though my gifts were used without care of recompense and my name forgotten, my aspect ignored.

No more must I wait. That much is true. The bargain must be kept or the well shall grow dry. Would you drink water or dust? The bargain must be kept or else there shall be dust.

What is that bargain? Simple enough—give credit where credit is due. Do not forget, I am She who opens the door, though I cannot and will not make you walk through it."

The Muse

Epilogue

Marisse

Red berries and white
Evergreen and holly
Snow falls through the broken windows
As She sleeps
Beauty and sadness
The madness of desire stilled
No breath remaining
But blue frost on her lips
The kiss of a poor lost prince
Winter's repose
His cloak lies over her
A spell she cannot deny.

Her dreams are of blood
And of those who wander
In hunger and in despair
She cannot deny
The anguish which lifts the spirit
And would break the chains
Of those whose own dark hearts
Would bind a world to pain
And keep it blind
To its own true
And dreadful power.

The tolling of the bell
Which would mark her freedom
Would sound their own ending.
The kiss which wakes her at the last
Coming not from her own
But from a soul

Brave and true
And sharp as any blade
A man in black
And with a heart bright as the sun.

Dark eyes open
Filled with the anguish of
A hundred thousand years
The land responds
And blooms
Winter blossoms
Red and white
As though blood spilled on snow
Gold at the center
The gold of risen kings
The sacrifice of the old year to the new
Her song goes out
Her call
And others wake
Polish their swords
And disappear into the night.

The time has come
The time is over
Bloody business ahead
The lady to reign again.

A figure lays full length on a great stone in a chapel long fallen into ruin. The roof is gone and many of the walls, leaving broken stone columns and the remnants of old archways, doors through which the light and the unquiet world pours. Ivy twists and climbs, the growth of centuries, as what was once tame has grown wild and restless. Though stillness remains at the center of the chapel, a great silence, as though all lies bound up in a spell of ancient sleep.

She who is upon the stone does sleep, the secret origin of all the tales of spelled princesses and of dreaming curses, of glass coffins and wicked faeries. She is the legend of the one who waits the kiss of a prince, of Her one true love, in order to awaken at the last. She sleeps the sleep of death and not-death, the sleep of a Goddess whose worship has also long fallen into ruin, but who has not yet been completely forgotten, nor ever really could be.

We do not really know this Goddess, for She does not belong to this world. Even though the world She comes from is familiar enough to our own to be recognizable in some ways, perhaps an alternative history, an Earth that might have been. She comes from the Otherworld, from one of the many worlds born of countless possibilities, where She is the Muse and a Goddess linked to the sea. In this other world, She also happens to be the patron Goddess of France, just as their version of Joan of Arc was Her chosen one, a priestess of passion and the red tides of desire, of the sacred possession of war.

She is the keeper of the company, the blood warriors and protectors of France. Her flag is like a sea of blood, with a golden crown and lily imprinted upon it. She protects Her land above all else and calls those to Her service in that respect. She is mother to the living waters of France, and in Her world the revolution never came and the Kings of France yet bear Her name - or one of Her names anyway, for the name She has given to be used here, when She visits our world, is *Marisse*.

She says that Her *"stories are writ in blood, blood on the snow, and sweat and breath and sweet tears. My joys are pain and by pain the tearing agony of love lost and returned, of going far and unknowing of whether you shall ever see home again. I am not the home fires, the safe hearth, the table of familial cordiality. I am the meat snatched on the sly, the glass downed in an oath of promised hardship, knowing that perhaps death will come of it. Ah, but then what is death to the brave? It is as nothing, a passing shadow, a dream quick to fade.*

What lasts, what lingers, is the hunger in the blood, the thirst of the spirit, to do what has never been done before or, at least, the attempt made. I am hunger and I am thirst. I am the sleeper awakened, the soul of a people. Without me, they sleep, as your own kinspirits, the souls of nations, have slept. Awaken the kindred kind, the Gods and Goddesses of each land, and feed Them well. Hungry Gods may be most unkind.

The blood goes into the land and the spirits wake. They drink the blood, the blood they know, and they wake. Often, the blood is shed in war, in guardianship of the land, but not always. Some simply know to feed the land is to feed the Gods and to feed the Gods is to feed the people, the nation. If the Gods of a nation are strong, the nation is strong. Those who feed the Gods, their blood is known. The Gods come to them. They are bound together, protectors of land and people.

Jeanne d'Orleans was one such. Her blood was known. She was priestess of the blood. All who would serve as such wear the mark. Their blood is sworn. The land acts through them. The Gods know their names, their true names. So it has been and so it shall be. My story is the story of my nation."

Of course, our France is not quite the France of Marisse, just as our Earth is not the Earth She knows, yet each can affect each other, just as the storms of change pass from world to world, the transformations that they cause yielding similar results. For all worlds touch upon each other, and all the Gods and Goddesses may know each other, especially those who are alike in some fashion. And so we have Aphrodite, Cerridwen, Ariadne, and the Lady of the Lake—who, Herself, has more than one name—and we also have Marisse, a Goddess and aspect of the Muse who may visit us from another world.

When we open the way to other places, we will encounter other forms of divine expression, other Gods and Goddesses. The closer this world is to our own in history and culture, the more likely that those Gods and Goddesses will seem familiar in some respect and understandable to our sensibilities. For the core spark holds true across boundaries, across worlds, though the mask it takes on, the name and so the form changes from place to place, time to time. As those of Faery change from the guise of elves to aliens; what is essential about them does not change, even though their appearance does.

So what can we learn from a Goddess from a place not quite here?

Like Aphrodite, Marisse is also a goddess of the passion of love and the passion of war. She is a fierce goddess, never shrinking from the battle. Her echo in our own world lies not just in Aphrodite, but in *Marianne*, the female emblem of the French Revolution, in the unspeakable rage which gives rise to the violence and bloodshed that brings freedom to the land, no matter the cost. In this, She is a close kin to the Goddess of Freedom. But then, Freedom and the Muse must go hand-in-hand. Inspiration strikes and seeks expression and if you are not free then this expression may be repressed or destroyed. When you walk with the Muse, you need to have the freedom to walk.

The Museship of this Goddess is of a particular kind; She is a national Muse, the inspiration of a place, of a whole country. She is not as concerned with a poem or a painting or a piece of prose here and there, not unless it serves the purpose—the unfolding tale of a country, of its people and its places. Whatever rouses the fire within a people bears Her singular touch. Revolutionary poems, inflammatory articles, words and images that lead to action are the flavor of Marisse's inspiration.

But She is also a Muse of place, as we here in this world have Muses of place. If a lands vitality falls lax, its brightness dimmed, then the servants of the Muse of the land, Her warrior-poets, rouse the senses, call for change, re-write and re-invigorate the future. For countries can fall into despair as much as people. Countries can forget what they are and lose touch with their source, wandering onto the wrong path and clothing itself in the trappings of what it is not.

Every land has its story, its mythology if you will, embodied both within the land and within the people who live there. The beliefs of the society, of the country, are embodied in its stories. They play out through time and place, small stories that reflect great stories and great stories that reflect the greatest story, patterns within patterns. We all play a part in that.

Today's counties sometimes have the remnants of this idea in their patron Saints. The Gods and Goddesses who used to be patrons of a clan or a family or a country give clues to the inner nature of what They guard. The God and Goddess are, in some ways, *mother* and *father* to the nation and if a country is warlike, the God or Goddess that represents them is often a deity of war. If the core nature of a country is the pursuit of the Arts, then little less than the Muse will do. This doesn't mean that each country doesn't have their own Muse, but that the Muse might not be their patron.

The Muse of place knows that Her waters run deep, surging forth in wellsprings of power, often where real springs, rivers, or wells come into being, sacred sites often linked to the Unseen currents of power in the land. A similar river runs in the blood, including the blood of a family, a clan, a nation. Some families are wellsprings, pouring out gifts of fertile power and change. These families are often tied to the land and its wellsprings are much as their own. They are kin. They have shared their blood with the land and the land has shared blood with them.

Marisse says *"how else is family made? There is always blood. There must be blood."*

The life's blood of the Muse is a bright current, a vital force. It's a drink that we simply can't live without, either as individuals or as a people. We all choose what to make of it, what to make it into. It runs through the weave of each land, including those who live there and are bound to it. The current sparks and jangles, spits and flares, art and history spinning off in twirling stars, in the scales of the eternal serpent—not just names, dates, statistics, but a living history braided by people and place.

What a country believes of itself imparts to what it is and shall become and those beliefs are steeped in the past. The thread of the Muse works to pull it all together, an intimate part of the pattern. History does have a lot to do with the pattern, but not just written history. Myth, story, memory, symbols, songs, folklore, fashion, tradition all come together to make the life of a family, a people, a nation, the world.

What shall be our history? From where have we come and to where are we going? All, all remains in motion, even that which seemingly is set in stone.

Guided Meditation for the Muse

For this meditation, it can be completely dark except for the candle the reader will need or you can have a candle lit at the four Quarters. A statue of the Muse can be put on the altar or set in the middle of the room. Incense is also a good idea, especially one that is good at inducing a trance state.

Have everyone relax as best they can, doing some deep and calming breathing before the reader begins:

A pool is before you, a great lake, a sea, black and still. The night sky is filled with stars and each star lies reflected in the pool below. There is no sound here but my voice. No sound but that of your own breathing.

Concentrate on your breathing and on my voice. Let each breath make you feel more relaxed and calm. Let the quiet of this place seep into you, deep, dark, still. You are safe here. There is nothing to fear.

Calm, quiet, relaxed. Deep breaths, each one making you feel more at peace, more relaxed.

Still and silent, the water and stars are as one and you between them. You stand on the edge, yet you are not afraid. Let each breath carry you deeper as all of your earthly concerns drift away, no more.

There is no hurry here, nothing to do, nowhere to go. All you must do is breath, breath and relax. Relax. Deep. Dark. Still. Deep. Dark. Still.

The waters are still. The stars, quiet. All you hear is my voice and the sound of your own breathing. Slow and relaxed. Deep and still.

And now you are relaxed, the dark filling you up, the stillness a part of you. You are a part of the waters, one with the stars.

In the pool before you a ripple appears now, a shiver, a small circle of waves expanding gently outwards. The stars tremble, moved by unseen in the dark. There is a sense of expectation. Not fearful, just waiting.

In the distance, you can see a figure walking towards you now, a figure made all of shadows. She is graceful and sure, her feet moving on the surface of the black water, barely touching it.

As She approaches nearer you see that She is wearing a mask. What the mask reveals is as important as what the mask doesn't reveal. It will be different for everyone. Remember the mask.

When She reaches the shore, you realize that you do know Her, that you've always known Her. For She is the Muse, beautiful and dread, passionate and cold. She is the Muse and when She opens Her arms, stars tumble down Her gown, falling into the water below. They flash deep, lighting that which lies in the depths.

You hear Her voice, deep and soft, lovely and still:

You, I have waited for you. I have waited for you to hear. I have waited for you to speak, to speak with a voice all your own and no others.

For these are my Arts. These are my gifts, given freely no more. Though if you dare honor my name, reveal my face, then the door shall open and inspiration be yours.

What is it you are passionate about? It is your passion that shows the way.

What is it you cannot live without? Your life and the Art are one.

What is it you desire to bring to the world? You are mother and father to that which shall bear your name.

Look then. Look if you dare. Look into the waters, see into your heart, and know is reflected there…

(Be silent for a length of time so that all may look and have a vision.)

What you have seen are clues to your gift, the offering of the Muse. It's up to you to feel and to dare, to seize opportunity and open to inspiration. You must give form to passion so it may walk freely in the world. The world you must now begin to return to.

The darkness is growing now around the Lady, wrapping Her in shadow. Her mask has become blank, unwritten, unknown. She turns away, walking back the way She came. She disappears into the distance and a moment later a star arches across the heavens, finding a perfect reflection in the waters below.

It is time for you to go. Time for you to leave. Concentrate once more on your breathing, feeling it begin to quicken now. Each breath brings you closer to wakefulness, to movement. Each breath brings you back to the world you know. Deep breaths, filling you up with energy, with awareness.

Ten. The darkness beginning to lighten.

Nine. The sky turning faintly red and orange.

Eight. The red and orange giving way to gold.

Seven. The shadows pulling back.

Six. The gold transforming to white.

Five. The edge of the sun appearing on the horizon.

Four. Light shooting out in all directions.

Three. The light shines within.

Two. Never to be forgotten.

One. As you wake, aware of all you have seen and experienced.

It might be a good idea to write down what you remember while it is still fresh. This can be shared with the group or not. This is a beginning, a path to be followed, a means of expressing yourself and the power of the Muse. If you find a symbol or image that represents what you have seen, you can set that next to where you like to work on your Art. You can also do divination if you need further clarification of what you have seen.

Recommended Reading

The Artist's Way, A Spiritual Path to Higher Creativity by Julia Cameron

Finding Water, the Art of Perseverance by Julia Cameron

A Mythic Life, Learning to Live Our Greater Story by Jean Houston

Putting Your Passion Into Print by Arielle Eckstut and David Henry Sterry

Shadow Dance, Liberating the Power and Creativity of your Dark Side by David Richo

The War of Art, Break Through the Blocks and Win Your Inner Creative Battles by Steven Pressfield

"The poet's eye, in a fine frenzy rolling,
Doth glance from heaven to earth,
from earth to heaven;
And as imagination bodies forth
The forms of things unknown, the poet's pen
turns them into shapes, and gives
to airy nothing a local habitation and a name..."

A Midsummer-Night's Dream
William Shakespeare

"Eternity is in love with the creations of time."

William Blake

Index